D1259413

02/23
STRAND PRICE
FOR $5.00 EACH

7/18/85

MENTAL PRODIGIES

MENTAL PRODIGIES

An Enquiry into the Faculties of Arithmetical, Chess and Musical Prodigies, Famous Memorizers, Precocious Children and the Like, with Numerous examples of "Lightning" Calculations and Mental Magic

by

FRED BARLOW

GREENWOOD PRESS, PUBLISHERS
WESTPORT. CONNECTICUT

Published 1952 by the Philosophical Library, Inc.

Reprinted by permission of the Philosophical Library, Inc.

Reprinted in 1969 by Greenwood Press, Inc., 51 Riverside Avenue,
Westport, Conn. 06880

Library of Congress catalog card number 70-88982
ISBN 0-8371-2092-6

Printed in the United States of America

10 9 8 7 6 5 4 3 2

To
RON AND FRANK

CONTENTS

7

SECTION IV—MENTAL MAGIC

SECTION V—PSYCHOLOGICAL ASPECTS

PREFACE

THIS book has been written to satisfy the curiosity of the ever-growing public interested in abnormal mentalities and their practical manifestations. The author has devoted many years to a study of the subject and in his modest way he has to some extent been an exponent of some of the phenomena that he records.

Every endeavour has been made throughout the whole text to ensure accuracy both in fact and in the numerous arithmetical examples that are given, but complete facts in many cases have been impossible to come by and it might be too bold to claim infallibility in all the figures. If any inaccuracies should be discovered it is, however, unlikely that they will seriously affect the general argument or the purpose for which the book was written.

The author expresses his thanks to the publishers and authors who have given permission for reproduction of extracts from books mentioned in the Bibliography at the end of the volume, the individual references to which are indicated by numbers throughout the text. He is pleased, also, to have this opportunity of acknowledging the constructive criticism and assistance rendered by Mr. W. H. Johnson of the Scientific and Technical Department of Messrs. Hutchinson & Co. (Publishers) Ltd.

FRED BARLOW.

Tanworth-in-Arden
October, 1951.

In this reprinting the opportunity has been taken to incorporate a few corrections and amendments to the text.

F.B.

May, 1952.

INTRODUCTION

FROM time immemorial, unusual specimens of humanity have attracted and amazed the wise men of the ages, but it is only during the last century or so that the study of mental prodigies has been conducted on a scientific basis. Even in the present progressive age, our knowledge of these gifted individuals is still in its infancy and much remains to be done in the way of the correlation and consideration of attested records.

The Oxford Dictionary describes a prodigy as something out of the ordinary course of nature. This is a very comprehensive definition which might apply equally well to Socrates and his *Daemon* or a calculating boy with his arithmetical marvels.

The first part of this book will be devoted mainly to the description and discussion of the results produced by what have been variously termed arithmetical prodigies, calculating boys, and other such arithmetical names. Following the procedure adopted by Dr. Mitchell, by an "arithmetical prodigy" we shall mean a person who shows unusual ability in mental arithmetic, or mental algebra, especially when this ability develops at an early age and without external aids or special tuition. We shall use the word "calculator" in the sense of "mental calculator", as a synonym for "arithmetical prodigy", and shall mean by "calculation", "mental calculation" unless the contrary is clearly indicated by the context. All problems described as being solved by an arithmetical prodigy will be understood to be done mentally, unless otherwise indicated.

We shall want to know all there is to be known of these persons—their environment, heredity, education (if any), the times taken to supply the answers and the nature of the problems tackled, etc. Above all, we shall try to discover *how* they do it and, for this reason, much of the space will be occupied by the necessary data. The reader need not be alarmed by the word "mathematical". It may occasionally be used where the word "arithmetical" would be more correct and in any case no advanced mathematical knowledge will be required to follow the arguments in these pages.

In an endeavour to include a brief reference to all the better-known calculators, and others not so well-known, more space has been taken than was originally intended. This is not altogether regrettable, as it is believed to be the first time this information has been gathered together in this way.

Investigations will not be confined to calculating prodigies. We shall want to devote some time to the study of associated subjects—in particular, to those persons possessing, to an unusual extent, the faculty of memory and also to musical and chess prodigies, men of genius, and precocious children.

We shall want to know how far these gifts may be developed and to what extent the average individual may be able to perform some of these, apparently extraordinary, mental operations. A consideration of the methods employed in memorizing and the use of mnemonics will prove of assistance in this direction.

Section IV of the book is given to a study of the routines frequently employed by magicians in their demonstrations of mental magic. This will assist the reader in making comparisons between the natural gift possessed by most calculators and the results obtained by the trained magician who has come to be known as a mentalist—we shall employ this comprehensive word to indicate the magical demonstrator. There is a very close resemblance between the effects produced by mental prodigies and those demonstrated by specialists in mental magic and for this reason both these aspects of figuring have been dealt with at some length.

It has been truly said that the subject of mental prodigies has frequently been the occasion of a considerable amount of uncritical observation. It will be our endeavour to avoid the awe and credulity with which they have been regarded in certain quarters and to steer clear of the other extreme of bigoted criticism—strange as it may seem, there are many who contemptuously dismiss many of the achievements of mental prodigies as so much deliberate trickery.

It will, of course, be realized that it is now quite impossible to give anything approaching a complete history of mental prodigies, as no reliable information is available prior to the early part of the eighteenth century. It is possible, however, to provide a reasonably representative account of the most significant features concerning prodigies from then onwards and the information thus made available may assist in the construction of a framework of facts helpful to future investigators.

SECTION I
ARITHMETICAL PRODIGIES

CHAPTER I
HISTORY AND DATA

"We carry within us the wonders, we seek without us.
There is all Africa, and her prodigies in us."
SIR THOMAS BROWNE.

THE first attempt to give a complete account and bibliography of calculators was made by E. W. Scripture (Bib. 2) in Vol. IV of the *American Journal of Psychology* in 1891. The author's indebtedness to this source and to a long article by Frank D. Mitchell (Bib. 3) in Vol. XVIII of the same journal in 1907 is gratefully acknowledged. The courtesy of the Editor of the *American Journal of Psychology* has made it possible to give extended information of the earlier calculators from these reliable channels. F. W. H. Myers, who died on 17 January, 1901, in his posthumous classic *Human Personality* (Bib. 4) made many references to the work of Scripture.

Scripture is helpful in that he gives copious references to the various authorities from whom he obtained much of his information and the most important of these are included in the Bibliography in this volume. Frank D. Mitchell refers extensively to the authorities quoted by Scripture. Both these investigators derived considerable assistance from *A Memoir of Zerah Colburn*, written by himself, Springfield, Mass., 1833 (Bib. 5); a comprehensive account by Bidder in the *Proceedings of the Institution of Civil Engineers*, Vol. XV, session 1855–1856, London 1856, pp. 251 ff. On Mental Calculation (Bib. 6); *Chambers' Edinburgh Journal* 1847 (Bib. 7) and from articles by various writers in the *Spectator* 1878 and 1879 (Bib. 8).

It only remains to add that the list of calculators in this chapter, will be given in chronological order, leaving the question of analysis and discussion to later chapters.

JEDEDIAH BUXTON (1702–1772), a native of Derbyshire, was a man of little intelligence (Bib. 2). It is said that at maturity, apart from arithmetic, he had the mentality of a child of ten, in spite of the fact that his father and grandfather were men of some education. His arithmetical gifts do not appear to have attracted attention until he had reached the age of twelve. It is typical of his outlook on life to record that he could give a detailed account of the free beer he had consumed over a period of many years from the age of twelve.

Buxton was particularly slow in calculation but he had an amazing memory and could retain long numbers for many weeks. Occasionally, his mental calculations kept him occupied for several months. *The Gentleman's Magazine* (Bib. 9) gives the testimony of two witnesses as follows:

"I proposed to him the following random question: In a body whose three sides are 23,145,789 yards, 5,642,732 yards, and 54,965 yards, how many cubical eighths of an inch? After once naming the several figures distinctly, one after another, in order to assure himself of the several dimensions and fix them in his mind, without more ado he fell to work amidst more than one hundred of his fellow-labourers, and after leaving him about five hours, on some necessary concerns (in which time I calculated it with my pen) at my return, he told me he was ready: Upon which, taking out my pocketbook and pencil, to note down his answer, he asked which end I would begin at, for he would direct me either way . . . I chose the regular method . . . and in a line of twenty-eight figures, he made no hesitation nor the least mistake."

"He will stride over a piece of land or a field, and tell you the contents of it, almost as exact as if you measured it by the chain. . . . He measured in this manner the whole lordship of Elmton, of some thousand acres . . . and brought the contents, not only in acres, rods and perches, but even in square inches . . . for his own amusement he reduced them to square hair-breadths, computing (I think) 48 to each side of the inch."

On one occasion Buxton mentally squared a number of 39 figures, in $2\frac{1}{2}$ months. His methods were primitive and very clumsy; to multiply by 378, in one instance, he multiplied successively by 5, 20, and 3 to get 300 times the number, then by 5 and 15 to get a second partial product, and finally by 3 to complete the operation. Thus, instead of adding two zeros to multiply by 100, he multiplied first by 5 and then by 20. This fact, together with his slowness, shows pretty clearly that his methods were of counting rather than multiplication, though we are told that he had learned the multiplication table in his youth. He was able to calculate while working or talking, and could handle two problems at once, without confusion. At a sermon or play Buxton seems to have paid no attention to the speaker's meaning but to have amused himself by counting the words spoken, or the steps taken in a dance, or by some long self-imposed calculation. The most stirring event in his otherwise quiet and obscure life was a visit to London in 1754, when he was introduced to the Fellows of the Royal Society, who asked him a number of questions to prove his ability, all of which he answered to their entire satisfaction and surprise. Beyond this he never left his birth-place, where he died in 1772.

Tom Fuller (1710–1790), (Bib. 2, 3), "the Virginia calculator" came from Africa as a slave when about fourteen years old. We first hear of him as a calculator at the age of seventy, or thereabouts, when among other problems, he reduced a year and a half to seconds in about two minutes, and 70 years, 17 days, 12 hours to seconds in about a minute and a half, correcting the result of his examiner, who had failed to take account of the leap years. This is an instance where it took a calculator longer to work out a simple problem than it did to answer one more difficult. This frequently occurs and the explanation would seem to be associated with the nature of the subconscious response. Conscious effort is occasionally more of a hindrance than a help. Fuller also found the sum of a simple geometrical progression, and multiplied mentally two numbers of nine figures each. He began his application to figures by counting up to ten and proceeded up to one hundred. He was entirely illiterate.

ANDRÉ MARIE AMPÈRE (1775–1836), (Bib. 4), like Safford (see pp. 42–45), showed all-round precocity, a wide range of interests, and an omnivorous memory. His name will always be associated with the measurement of electric current. He learned counting at the age of three or four, by means of pebbles. It is stated, that he was so fond of this diversion that, on one occasion, he used for purposes of calculation pieces of a biscuit given him after three days' strict diet.

As soon as he could read he devoured every book that fell into his hands. His father allowed him to follow his own inclination and contented himself with furnishing the necessary books. History, travel, poetry, romances and philosophy interested him almost equally. His principal study was an encyclopædia, in twenty volumes folio. This colossal work was completely and deeply engraved on his mind.

Arago, in eulogizing Ampère, said: "His mysterious and wonderful memory astonishes me a thousand times less than that force united to flexibility which enables the mind to assimilate without confusion, after reading in alphabetical order, matter so astonishingly varied." Half a century afterwards, he would repeat with perfect accuracy long passages from the encyclopædia relating to blazonry, falconry, etc.

At the age of eleven years the child had conquered elementary mathematics and had studied the application of algebra to geometry. The parental library was not sufficient to supply him with further books, so his father took him to Lyons, where he was introduced to higher analysis. He learned according to his fancy, and his thought gained in vigour and originality. Mathematics interested him above everything. At eighteen he studied the *Mechanique Analytique* of Lagrange, nearly all of whose calculations he repeated. He said often that he knew at that time as much mathematics as he ever did.

In 1793, his father was killed by the revolutionaries and young Ampère was completely paralysed by the blow. Rousseau's botanical letters and a chance glance at Horace roused him, after more than a year, from an almost complete idiocy and he gave himself up with unrestrained zeal to the study of plants and the Augustan poets. At the age of twenty-one his heart suddenly opened to a new passion and then began the romantic story of his love, which is preserved in his *Amorum* and his letters. Ampère became professor of mathematics, chemistry, writer on probabilities, poet, psychologist, metaphysician, member of the Academy of Sciences of Paris, discoverer of fundamental truths of electro-dynamics and a defender of the unity of structure in organized beings.

Just as he began by learning completely the encyclopædia of the eighteenth century, he remained encyclopædic all his life, and his last labours were on a plan for a new encyclopædia. It is strange, and also unfortunate, that we have so little specific information regarding the calculating ability of this great mathematician. His later achievements so overshadowed his earlier gift that his biographers have little to say about it. A genius of his knowledge and experience could, undoubtedly, have afforded much useful information but he seems to have taken his gift for calculating very much as a matter of course, probably because of his mental activities in so many other directions.

CARL FRIEDRICH GAUSS (1777–1855), (Bib. 2, 3, 4) was born in Braunschweig and came of a poor family. A maternal uncle, however, was a man of considerable mathematical and mechanical talent. When not quite three years old, Gauss, according to an anecdote told by himself, followed mentally a calculation of his father's, relative to the wages of some of his workmen, and detected a mistake in the amount.

The genius of Gauss began to show itself at an early age. With the assistance of friends and of persons of the nobility he was enabled to get a school education. At the age of eleven, he entered the gymnasium where he mastered the classical languages with incredible rapidity. He also distinguished himself in mathematics. It is said that a new professor of mathematics handed back to the thirteen-year-old Gauss his first exercise with the remark that it was unnecessary for such a mathematician to attend his lectures in the future. The Grand Duke of the Duchy of Brunswick, hearing of his talent, sent for him. The court was entertained by the calculations of the fourteen-year-old boy, but the Duke recognized the genius and gave him his support.

As is the case with Ampère, it is to be regretted that we have not more complete accounts of his early calculations, but here also his later achievements so completely occupied the scientific world that less attention was paid to his calculating powers. Scripture claims that if he had had the misfortune to have been gifted with nothing else, he would probably have distinguished himself as did the calculators Dase and Mondeux. He might even have proclaimed himself in the Colburn fashion, as a miraculous exception from the rest of mankind; as it was, he was the greatest mathematician of the century!

After leaving the gymnasium in 1795, he entered the University of Göttingen and from 1807 until his death he held the directorship of the Göttingen Observatory. As early as 1795, he discovered the method of the least squares, and in 1796 he invented the theory of the division of the circle. In 1801, when he was twenty-four, his *Disquisitiones Arithmeticæ* was published. The work was immediately recognized as a milestone in the history of the theory of numbers. From this point on, his life was a series of most brilliant discoveries till his death at Göttingen in 1855.

Gauss was always distinguished for his power of reckoning and was able to carry on difficult investigations and extensive numerical calculations with incredible ease. His unsurpassed memory for figures aroused the astonishment of those who met him. If he did not know the answer to a problem immediately, he stored it up for future solution. He was able to give at once, or after a very short pause, the properties of each of the first two thousand numbers. He had always in his mind the first decimal of the logarithm of every number, and used them for approximate estimates while calculating mentally. He would often pursue a calculation for days and even weeks and—what distinguishes him from most other calculators—during such a calculation he continually invented new methods and new artifices.

ZERAH COLBURN (1804–1840) (Bib. 2, 3, 5, 10), the son of a farmer, was born at Cabot, Vermont, U.S.A. on 1 September, 1804. Signs of his unusual powers appeared at an early age. It is said that the discovery was accidentally made, when he was six years old, by his father, who was much surprised to hear him repeating the product of several numbers, although at the time he had received instruction only at a small country school, whose curriculum did not include writing, or ciphering.

From what Colburn says of himself in his *Memoir* (Bib. 5) (published in 1833) his early efforts were of a very simple nature. His father heard him repeating parts of the multiplication table, such as "5 times 7 are 35", "6 times 8 are 48" and so on. It is stated that on being asked the product of 13 × 97, he gave the answer immediately.

The next step in Colburn's progress was a visit, accompanied by his father, to Montpelier, Vermont, where he gave several exhibitions. Of his performances here we have only three specimens and they are more illustrative of Yankee shrewdness than of calculating ability, *e.g.* "Which is the most, twice twenty-five or twice five and twenty (2 × 25 or 2 × 5 + 20)? Which is the most, six dozen dozen or half a dozen dozen (6 × 12 × 12 or 6 × 12)? It is stated too that someone asked how many black beans would make five white ones. His answer was "Five, if you skin them".

Practically the whole of the information given by Scripture and Mitchell concerning Colburn has been taken from the calculator's *Memoir* but many of these calculations were confirmed at the time in various periodicals, published in England and the U.S.A. and there is every evidence to indicate that the information given in the *Memoir* is substantially correct.

At Boston, when still only six years of age, he gave further public exhibitions. "Questions in multiplication of two or three places of figures, were answered with much greater rapidity than they could be solved on paper. Questions involving an application of this rule, seemed to be perfectly adapted to his mind". The extraction of the roots of exact squares and cubes was done with very little effort; and what has been considered by the mathematicians of Europe an operation for which no rule existed, viz., finding the factors of numbers, was performed by him, although "questions in addition, subtraction and division were done with less facility, on account of the more complicated and continued effort of the memory." In regard to the higher branches of arithmetic, he claimed that he had no rules peculiar to himself, but if the common process laid down in the books were pointed out, he would carry on the process very readily in his head.

"Supposing I have a corn-field, in which there are 7 acres, having 17 rows to each acre: 64 hills to each row, 8 ears on a hill, and 150 kernels on an ear; how many kernels on the corn-field? *Answer:* 9,139,200."

In June 1811, he visited Portsmouth (U.S.A.) and answered the following: "Admitting the distance between Concord and Boston to be 65 miles, how many steps must I take in going this distance, allowing that I go three feet at a step?" The answer, 114,400 was given in ten seconds. "How many seconds in eleven years?" The answer that was given in four seconds was 346,896,000. (No allowance was made for leap years. The method of determining leap years is given on pages 185 and 187. Where mention is made, in a problem, of a number of years and not specified by date it is not determinable exactly how many leap years they include, *e.g.* the period of eleven years from 1 January, 1897, to 31 December, 1907, contained only one leap year, whereas the five years from 1 January, 1904, to 31 December, 1908, contained two leap years.) "What number multiplied by itself will produce 998,001?" *Answer,* in less than four seconds, 999. (*See* Appendix III, page 248.)

The following summer (1812) Zerah's father took him to England and made efforts to secure the patronage of the nobility. At a meeting there "he undertook and succeeded in raising the number 8 to the sixteenth power, 281,474,976,710,656. He was then tried as to other numbers, consisting of one figure, all of which he raised as high as the tenth power, with so much facility that the person appointed to take down the results was obliged to enjoin him not to be so rapid. With respect to numbers of two figures, he would raise some of them to the sixth, seventh and eighth power, but not always with equal facility; for the larger the products became the more difficult he found it to proceed. He was then asked the square root of 106,929 and before the number could be written down he immediately answered 327. He was then requested to name the cube root of 268,336,125 and with equal facility and promptness he replied 645."

It had been asserted that 4,294,967,297 ($=2^{32} + 1$) was a prime number. Euler detected the error by discovering that it was equal to $641 \times 6,700,417$. The same number was proposed to this child, who found out the factors "by the mere operation of his mind". Scripture is sceptical as to the truth of this statement which appeared in the *Memoir*, but at the same time quotes from Prime's *Life of S. B. Morse*, New York, 1875, page 68, to the effect that Morse met Zerah in London, and a friend of Morse had written, "There was some great arithmetical question, I do not exactly know what, which he solved as soon as it was put to him, though for several years it had baffled the skill of some of the first professors".

The father and son, after a visit to Ireland and Scotland, returned to London. In 1814 they proceeded to Paris but little interest appears ·to have been taken there in his calculations. The comment on this, in the *Memoir*, reads, "Whether it were principally owing to the native frivolity and lightness of the French people, or to the painful effect produced by the defeat of their armies and the restoration of the exiled Louis XVIII, cannot be correctly stated: probably it was owing to the former".

He was introduced to and examined by members of the French Academy, among whom was Laplace. The *Memoir* continues: "Three months had now elapsed that he had not been exhibited, but had given his attention to study; even in this short space it was observable that he had lost in the rapidity of his computations." Before long his calculating power left him entirely.

By the exertions of Washington Irving, at that time in Paris, the boy obtained admission to the Lyceum Napoleon (or Royal College of Henri IV). Zerah gives an interesting account of this institution, which was under strict military discipline, and also of Westminster School, in which he was placed on his return to England.

Financial straits suggested to the father the possibility of the stage as a career and Zerah made an unsuccessful attempt at acting. Thereafter, in 1821, he started a private school but gave this up in little more than a year. After his return to America, he joined the Congregational Church but soon went over to the Methodists and began to hold religious meetings. He was ordained deacon, and laboured thenceforth as an itinerant preacher till, in 1835, he was appointed "Professor of the Latin, Greek, French and Spanish languages, and English classical literature" in a seminary styled the Norwich University. Here he died at the age of 35, leaving a wife and three children.

Colburn possessed bodily as well as mental peculiarities. His father and great-grandmother had a supernumerary digit on each hand and each foot. Zerah and three brothers possessed these extra members, while they were wanting in two brothers and two sisters. The calculator Arumogam (*see p.* 54) was also equipped like the man of Gath, mentioned in the Bible (I. Chronicles xx, 6) whose "fingers and toes were four and twenty, six on each hand and six on each foot". A portrait of Colburn was made in Philadelphia in 1810, and placed in the museum. It is reputed that Gall, who examined the boy without any previous intimation of his character "readily discovered on the sides of the eyebrows certain protuberances and peculiarities which indicated the presence of a faculty for computation".

The following are further questions, put to him at various times, which have been taken from several sources:

"Give the square of 999,999?" After hesitating a little, he replied 999,998,000,001. He was then asked to multiply the answer twice by 49 and once by 25: a task which he accomplished successfully, though the answer consists of seventeen figures. (*See* Appendix III, page 248.)

"Name the cube root of 413,993,348,677?" To this he gave the correct answer (7453) in five seconds.

"How many times would a coach wheel, 12 ft. in circumference, turn round in 256 miles, and how many minutes are there in 48 years?" To the first he gave the answer in two seconds (112,640) and to the second before the question could be written down—25,228,800 and added that the number of seconds in the same period was 1,513,728,000. On another occasion he was asked the number of seconds in 2,000 years and gave the answer 63,072,000,000. (These answers do not take account of leap years).

When asked to give the factors of 36,083 he immediately replied that it had none which, in fact, is the case. Other numbers were indiscriminately proposed to him and he invariably succeeded in giving the correct answers. If any number consisting of six or seven places of figures was proposed, he would determine easily and quickly, all the factors of which it was composed. This singular mental faculty, therefore, extended not only to the raising of powers, but also to the extraction of the square and cube roots of the numbers proposed.

Many persons tried to obtain a knowledge of the method by which he was able to answer with so much facility and accuracy the questions put to him, but without success. He positively declared that he was unable to tell how the answers came into his mind. That his process of operation was other than the usual mode of proceeding was evident, for he was entirely ignorant of the common rules of arithmetic at this time and could not, it is stated, perform upon paper a simple sum on multiplication or division.

In the extraction of roots and the mentioning of factors, he gave the answers so promptly as not to admit of any lengthy operation taking place in his mind, when it would require, according to the ordinary method of solution, a very difficult and laborious calculation.

In writing his *Memoir* Zerah carried out a plan which his father and friends had had in view long before. The *Memoir* contains a great deal of information regarding his unusual powers. In fact, Colburn is one of the few calculators concerning whom considerable data are available. These particulars, however, do not include much information regarding the time taken by Colburn on his calculations in the early stages of his career. The only series of problems, whose times he gives us, dates from 1811, before he was seven years old and so is hardly typical of his performances some years later, when he was in his prime. In his early years, his calculations were accompanied by certain bodily contortions, similar to those of St. Vitus's dance. They seem to have passed away rather early; Colburn himself had no recollection of them and mentions them simply on the authority of persons who saw him "when quite a child".

GEORGE PARKER BIDDER (1805–1878) (Bib. 2, 3, 4, 6), "the elder Bidder", was born at Moreton Hamstead, in Devonshire, where his father carried on a small business as a stone-mason.

At the early age of four, Bidder showed a most extraordinary ability for calculation and was exhibited as a prodigy. Nevertheless, strange as it seems, at the age of six, he learned from an elder brother to count to 10 and then to 100. This was the only formal instruction in figures that he ever received. From counting by units to counting by 10's, and then by 5's, was a natural development. He then set about learning the multiplication table up to 10 × 10, with the aid of shot, marbles, etc., until, as he expressed it, the numbers up to 100 became his friends, and he knew all about their relations and acquaintances. A year or so later, his readiness in solving simple problems, mentioned in his hearing attracted attention and he acquired a considerable local reputation. Concerning the early days, Bidder writes:

"I amused myself by repeating the process (of counting up to 100), and found that by stopping at 10, and repeating that every time, I counted up to 100 much quicker than by going through the series. I counted up to 10, then to 10 again = 20, 3 times 10 = 30, 4 times 10 = 40, and so on. This may appear to you a simple process, but I attach the utmost importance to it, because it made me perfectly familiar with numbers up to 100 . . . at this time I did not know one written or printed figure from another, and my knowledge of language was so restricted, that I did not know there was such a word as 'multiply'; but having acquired the power of counting up to 100 by 10 and by 5, I set about, in my own way, to acquire the multiplication table. This I arrived at by getting peas, or marbles, and at last I obtained a treasure in a small bag of shot. I used to arrange them in squares, of 8 on each side, and then on counting them throughout I found that the whole number amounted to 64. By that process I satisfied my mind, not only as a matter of memory, but as a matter of conviction, that 8 times 8 were 64; and that fact once established has remained there undisturbed until this day. In this way I acquired the whole multiplication table up to 10 times 10; beyond which I never went; it was all that I required."

Most of his time as a child was spent with an old blacksmith. On one occasion somebody by chance mentioned a sum and the boy astonished the bystanders by giving the answer correctly. "They went on to ask me up to two places of figures, 13 times 17, for instance. That was rather beyond me at the time, but I had been accustomed to reason on figures, and I said 13 times 17 means 10 times 10, plus 10 times 7, plus 10 times 3 and 3 times 7 . . ."

While remaining at the forge he received no instruction in arithmetic beyond desultory scraps of information derived from persons who came to test his powers, and who often in doing so gave him new ideas and encouraged the further development of his peculiar faculty, until he obtained a mastery of figures that appeared almost incredible. "By degrees I got on until the multiple arrived at thousands. Then . . . it was explained to me that 10 hundreds meant 1000. Numeration beyond that point is very simple in its features: 1000 rapidly gets up to 10,000 and 20,000, as it is simply 10 or 20 repeated over again, with thousands at the end, instead of nothing. So by degrees I became familiar with the numeration table, up to a million. From two places of figures I got to three places; then to four places of figures, which took me up, of course, to tens of millions; then I ventured to five and six places of figures, which I could eventually treat with great facility and, as already mentioned, on one occasion I went through the task of multiplying 12 places of figures by 12 figures, but it was a great and distressing effort."

Before long Bidder was taken about the country by his father for the purpose of exhibition. This was so profitable for the father that the boy's education was entirely neglected.

Even at the age of ten he was only just learning to write; figures he could not make.

Some of the questions he answered at this period were the following: "Suppose a cistern capable of containing 170 gallons, to receive from one cock 54 gallons, and at the same time to lose by leakage 30 gallons in one minute. In what time will the said cistern be full?" "How many drops are there in a pipe of wine, supposing each cubic inch to contain 4685 drops, each gallon 231 inches and 126 gallons in a pipe?" "In the cube of 36, how many times 1728?" Among others, the famous Herschel came in 1817 to see the "Calculating Boy".

Shortly afterwards he was sent to school for a time. Later, he was privately instructed and then attended the University of Edinburgh, obtaining the mathematical prize in 1822. After that he entered the Ordnance Survey and then was employed by the Institution of Civil Engineers. He was engaged in several engineering works of importance and, it is claimed, should be regarded as the founder of the London telegraphic system. His greatest work was the construction of the Victoria Docks, London. Bidder was engaged in most of the great railway contests in Parliament and was accounted "the best witness that ever entered a committee room". He was a prominent member, Vice-President, then President of the Institution of Civil Engineers. In his later years there was no appreciable diminution in Bidder's powers of retaining statistics in his memory and of dealing rapidly with figures.

The fact that Bidder became a highly educated man and one of the leading engineers of his time; that his powers increased rather than diminished with age and, above all, that he has given a clear and trustworthy account of how he obtained and exercised his talent, renders his testimony of the highest worth and provides the solution of many of the problems met with in the cases of Dase, Colburn and others. Indeed, he seems to complete just what is lacking in each case. Dase never gave a good account of the way in which he worked; Colburn could not till later explain his methods and then only in the clumsy way to be expected from a young man of little education; finally, just the part we cannot understand in Buxton is here explained.

In 1814, a witness to his powers stated, he displayed great facility in the mental handling of numbers, multiplying readily and correctly two figures by two, but failing in attempting numbers of three figures. The same witness was present at an examination of the boy in 1816 by several Cambridge men. The first question was a sum in simple addition, two rows with twelve figures in each row and the boy gave the correct answer at once. After more than an hour, the question was asked, "Do you remember the sum in addition I gave you?" He repeated the twenty-four figures with one or two mistakes. At that time he could not explain the processes by which he worked out long and intricate sums. It is evident that in the course of two years his powers of memory and calculation must have been gradually developed.

This development seems to have been steady. The following series shows the increasing rapidity with which the answers came:

1816 (ten years of age): "What is the compound interest on £4444 for 4444 days at 4½% per annum?" *Answer*, in 2 minutes, £2434 16s. 5¼d.

1817 (still ten years of age): "How long would a cistern 1 mile cube be filling, if receiving from a river 120 gallons per minute, without intermission?" *Answer*, in 2 minutes, 14,300 years, 285 days, 12 hours, 46 minutes. (The reader may like to work out this sum to ascertain whether due account has been taken of leap-years!)

1818 (eleven years of age): "Divide 468,592,413,563 by 9076." *Answer*, within 1 minute, 51,629,838.

1818 (twelve years of age): "If the pendulum of a clock vibrates the distance of $9\frac{3}{4}$ inches in a second of time, how many inches will it vibrate in 7 years, 14 days, 2 hours, 1 minute, 56 seconds, each year being 365 days, 5 hours, 48 minutes, 55 seconds?" *Answer*, in less than a minute, $2,165,625,744\frac{3}{4}$ inches.

1819 (thirteen years of age): "Find the number whose cube less 19 multiplied by its cube shall be equal to the cube of 6." *Answer*, instantly, 3.

Sir William Herschel put the following question: "Light travels from the sun to the earth in 8 minutes, and the sun being 98,000,000 miles off, if light would take 6 years and 4 months travelling at the same rate from the nearest fixed star, how far is that star from the earth, reckoning 365 days and 6 hours to each year, and 28 days to each month?" *Answer*, 40,633,740,000,000 miles.

Bidder and Colburn met in Derbyshire and underwent a comparative examination. Colburn in his *Memoir* (p. 175) says of this meeting:

"Some time in 1818, Zerah was invited to a certain place, where he found a number of persons questioning the Devonshire boy. He (Bidder) displayed great strength and power of mind in the higher branches of arithmetic. He could answer some questions that the American boy would not like to undertake, but he was unable to extract the roots and find the factors of numbers."

It would appear from this that Bidder's mind was not strongly turned in the direction of this class of problems until after this meeting with Colburn, but that once he became interested in them he soon outstripped his rival.

Professor Elliott, of Liverpool, who knew Bidder from the time they were fellow-students in Edinburgh, said he was a man of first-rate business ability and of rapid and clear insight into what was financially sound, especially in railway matters.

The Bidder family seems to have been distinguished for mental traits resembling George Bidder's in some part or another. George was noted for his amazing mathematical ability and his great memory. One of his brothers was an excellent mathematician and an actuary of the Royal Exchange Life Assurance Office. An elder brother was a Unitarian minister. This brother was not remarkable as an arithmetician, but he possessed the Bidder memory. He could quote almost any text in the Bible and give chapter and verse. He had long collected all the dates he could, not only of historical persons, but of everybody with whom he came in contact. To know when a person was born or married, is said to have been a source of gratification to him. One of George Bidder's nephews, at an early age, possessed remarkable mechanical ingenuity.

Most interesting of all was the partial transmission of his peculiar faculties to his eldest son, George Bidder Q.C. (usually known as "the younger Bidder", see p. 45) and through him to two grandchildren. His second son, was a first-class man in classics at Oxford and Fellow of his college. The elder Bidder, however, possessed the peculiar faculties of the family in such proportions that he far exceeded the others in calculating power.

The following are further representative specimens of the questions Bidder was asked to answer:

"If a flea springs 2 ft. 3 in. in every hop, how many hops must it take to go round the world, the circumference being 25,020 miles; and how long would it be performing the journey, allowing it to take 60 hops per minute, without intermission?" (*Answers:* 58,713,600 hops and 1 year, 314 days, 13 hours, 20 mins.)

The following problem was solved by Bidder in 40 seconds. "Supposing the ball at the top of St. Paul's Cathedral to be 6 ft. in diameter, what would the gilding cost at 3½d. per square inch?" (*Answer:* £237 10*s.* 1*d.*)

It took Bidder 80 seconds to answer this question. "Suppose a city to be illuminated with 9,999 lamps, each lamp to consume one pint of oil every four hours in succession; how many gallons would be consumed in forty years?" (*Answer:* 109,489,050 gallons.)

"Suppose the earth to consist of 971 million inhabitants, and suppose they die in 30 years and 4 months; how many have returned to dust since the time of Adam, computing it to be 5,850 years? Multiply the answer by 99."

It is related that on one occasion the proposer of a question was not satisfied with Bidder's answer. The boy said the answer was correct, and requested the proposer to work the sum over again. During the operation, Bidder said he was certain he was right, for he had worked the question in another way; and before the proposer found that he was wrong and Bidder right, he had solved the question by a third method.

Two days before his death, the query was suggested that taking the velocity of light at 190,000 miles a second, and the wave length of the red rays at 36,918 to an inch, how many of its waves must strike the eye in one second? His friend, producing a pencil, was about to calculate the result when Bidder said: "You need not work it out; the number of vibrations will be 444,433,651,200,000."

It would seem that Bidder's powers of mental calculation increased steadily, at least up to the beginning of his university days, if not later, and thereafter remained almost undiminished to the end of his life. Both in numerical calculations and in his study of mathematics, he was interested in general principles, practical applications, and striking properties, rather than in intricate analysis for its own sake, or calculations with numbers chosen merely for their length.

At Edinburgh he maintained a good class standing in mathematics, including differential and integral calculus, but only by hard study. In the solution of problems where special properties played a part he was equalled, if at all, only by such great calculator-mathematicians as Gauss and Ampère. In division his skill was considerable. In general, he did not cultivate his mechanical power much beyond the limits of its practical usefulness to him. In his lecture On Mental Calculation before the Institution of Civil Engineers (Bib. 6), Bidder has left us an excellent account of his methods of calculation. After taking a part in many important engineering works, he died at Dartmouth, 20 September, 1878, at the age of 72.

JOHANN MARTIN ZACHARIAS DASE (1824-1861) (Bib. 2, 3, 4), was born in Hamburg. Concerning his ancestry we have no information. He attended school at the age of $2\frac{1}{2}$ years, but attributed his powers to later practice and industry rather than to his early instruction. He seems to have been little more than a human calculating machine, able to carry on enormous calculations in his head, but nearly incapable of understanding the principles of mathematics, and of very limited ability outside his chosen field. In this respect he resembled Buxton: but in the rapidity and extent of his calculations he was incomparably superior to Buxton, or indeed any other calculator on record.

He spent most of his life in Hamburg, but made many journeys through Germany, Denmark and England, giving demonstrations in the most important towns. He began his public exhibitions at the age of 15 and continued them for a number of years.

He became acquainted with many of the learned men

of his time among, whom were Gauss, Schumacher, Petersen, and Encke. Petersen tried in vain to get into his head the first elements of mathematics. Schumacher referred to his extreme stupidity.

In 1840 Dase exhibited in Vienna. Whilst there he attended the lectures of Professor Strasznicky on the elements of mathematics. The Professor seems to have educated him to such a point that under the guidance of a good mathematician he could do scientific work.

Dase seemed anxious to use his powers in the service of science. In 1847 he reckoned the natural logarithms (seven places) of the numbers from 1 to 1,005,000, and was seeking a publisher. In reckoning on paper he seemed to possess all the accuracy of mental calculation, and added to this an incredible rapidity in doing long problems. In 1850, the largest hyperbolic table, as regards range, was published by him in Vienna and this was printed in the annals of the Vienna Observatory.

In 1850 Dase came to England to earn money by the exhibition of his powers. His experience in this country was very similar to that in Germany and his general obtuseness was the cause of some comment. He could not be trained to entertain the least idea of a proposition in Euclid and was never able to master any language other than that of his native land.

In 1849 Dase was desirous of making tables of factors and prime numbers from the 7th to the 10th million. On the recommendation of Gauss, the Academy of Sciences at Hamburg granted him support and Dase devoted himself to the task.

Gauss wrote to him in the following strain:

"With small numbers everybody that possesses any readiness in reckoning, sees the answer to such a question (the divisibility of a number) almost immediately and for greater numbers with more or less trouble. This trouble grows in an increasing relation as the numbers grow, until even an experienced reckoner may occupy himself for hours, or even days, over a single number. For still greater numbers, the solution by ordinary calculation becomes entirely impracticable. . . . You possess many of the requisite qualities (for establishing tables of factors) in an exceptional degree; a remarkable agility and quickness in handling arithmetical operations . . . and an invulnerable persistence and perseverance."

Up to his death in 1861, Dase had completed the tables of factors and prime numbers for the 7th million and also the 8th million, with the exception of a small portion. He thus spent only about eleven years on a task which very few men could have accomplished in a lifetime. The tables were completed by another computer (Rosenberg) and published, as far as the 9th million in 1862–1865.

Dase multiplied and divided large numbers in his head. Schumacher once gave him the number 79,532,853 to be multiplied by 93,758,479. From the moment in which the figures were given to the moment when he had written down the answer, which he had reckoned in his head, there elapsed 54 seconds. He multiplied mentally two numbers each of twenty figures in 6 minutes; of forty figures in 40 minutes and of one hundred figures in $8\frac{3}{4}$ hours. He extracted mentally the square root of a number of one hundred figures in 52 minutes. It is recorded that he could extract the square root of a sixty-figure number "in an incredibly short time".

Although Dase usually reckoned with astonishing accuracy, yet on at least two occasions his powers failed him. While he was in Hamburg, in 1840, he gave striking proofs of his talents, but at times made great mistakes. Luckily for him these happened seldom in comparison with his correct answers. In 1845, Schumacher wrote: "at a test which he was to undergo before me, he reckoned wrongly every time". This was explained as being due to a headache.

Dase seems to have retained his powers through life. He had one other notable gift which was probably related to his arithmetical powers; he could count objects with the greatest rapidity. With a single rapid glance, he could give the number of peas in a handful scattered on a table; and the ease and rapidity with which he could count sheep in a flock, books in a case, or the like, never failed to amaze the beholder. His powers in this direction were so far in advance of those of any other person of whom there is any record that he stands in a class by himself.

HENRI MONDEUX (1826–1862) (Bib. 2, 3, 4, 11) was the son of a poor wood-cutter, near Tours. Sent to tend sheep at the age of seven, he amused himself by playing with pebbles and thus learned mental arithmetic. At this period of life, pebbles seem to have been his signs for numbers, for he was ignorant of figures. He learned to execute arithmetical operations mentally and to create for his own use ingenious methods of simplification.

After long exercise at this calculation, he used to offer to persons he met to solve certain problems such as to tell how many hours or minutes were contained in the years of their ages. This awakened the interest of M. Jacoby, a schoolmaster at Tours, who sought him out. Jacoby proposed several problems and received immediate answers. Finding that the boy could neither read, write nor cipher, and that he had no acquaintance with fractions or any of the ordinary rules of arithmetic, he offered to instruct him.

Although in other matters he showed only mediocre intelligence, yet he was something more than a mere calculating machine, as is shown, for example, in his way of solving the following problem:

"In a public square there is a fountain containing an unknown quantity of water; around it stands a group of people with vessels capable of containing a certain unknown quantity. They draw at the following rate (each person drawing the same quantity): The first takes 100 quarts and one-thirteenth of the remainder; the second, 200 quarts and one-thirteenth of the remainder; the third 300 quarts and one-thirteenth, and so on until the fountain was emptied. How many quarts were there?"

In a few seconds he gave the answer; and this, according to Scripture, is the simple process by which he obtained it. Take the denominator of the fraction, subtract one; that gives the number of persons (12). Multiply that by the number of quarts taken by the first person—that is, by 100 —and you get the equal quantities taken by each (1200 quarts); multiply this quantity by the number of persons, and you get the quantity in the fountain (144,000 quarts).

It was claimed that Mondeux knew by heart the squares of all whole numbers under 100. To learn a number of 24 figures, divided into four 6-figure periods, required five minutes. He could solve a problem while attending to other things.

In 1840, M. Jacoby presented the boy to the Paris Academy of Science. Jacoby had taken note of the processes employed, and the boy was willing to tell them himself before a commission. On this occasion two questions were set him one of which was: "How many minutes are there in 52 years?" The child, who found the problem very simple, responded in a few moments: "52 years of 365 days each, are composed of 27,331,200 minutes and of 1,639,872,000 seconds".

A committee, including Arago and Cauchy, made an exhaustive examination of his powers and reported on the processes used by him: "At present, he easily executes in his head not only diverse operations of arithmetic but also, in many cases, the numerical resolution of equations. He invents processes, sometimes remarkable, to solve various questions which are ordinarily treated with the aid of algebra. More specifically, he finds powers of numbers by rules of his own discovery which are equivalent to special cases of the binomial theorem; he has worked out formulae for the summation of the squares, cubes etc., of the natural numbers and for arithmetical progression and other series. He solves simultaneous linear equations by a method of his own and sometimes equations of higher degree, especially where the root is a positive integer. He also solves such problems in indeterminate analysis as finding two squares whose difference is a given number." In spite, however, of his marvellous power of inventing and applying arithmetical methods, he did not answer the expectations of his friends, but sank into obscurity and died almost unknown.

Mrs. F. E. Leaning, in an interesting article on "Calculating Boys" in the *British Journal of Psychical Research* (Bib. 11), draws attention to some information about Mondeux, quoted by Dr. Osty from *La Grande Encyclopédie*. Jacoby, it seems, took his prodigy to a school of two hundred children at Lyons. These children had been trained in mental arithmetic by a special method. Mondeux here resolved all the numerical questions put to him, immediately upon hearing them, to the admiration of all hearers. The headmaster, however, asked that as a sequel his own pupils should be submitted to similar tests. Some fifty of the two hundred pupils present replied with the same exactitude and rapidity as Mondeux had done. This leads the writer in the *Encyclopédie* to remark that it is not difficult to develop the faculty of mental calculation in children. As Mrs. Leaning points out, however, there are evidently great diversities in this direction, since the whole school had been trained and practised, but only a proportion reached Mondeux's ability and he had had no training at all.

Mrs. Leaning suggests an interesting theme for discussion when she writes: "I have been informed by a teacher who had had special experience in the education of slow and backward children, that she was surprisingly successful in getting them to work sums mentally. In respect of other subjects some of these children gave markedly better results when in her own vicinity than when she was away from them."

This kind of observation throws a light, perhaps, from the psychological angle, which is worth more consideration than it has received. What if the dull child—dull at learning to read and write, that is—is simply a good recipient, or percipient, of mental impressions, whose subconscious predominates over his conscious brain? All persons who have the abnormal gifts that we call "psychic" display them in a fluctuating and periodical way. Rarely are they steadfast lifelong possessions. And the mathematical prodigy is a typical instance.

VITO MANGIAMELE (*b.* 1827) (Bib. 2, 3). In the year 1837, Mangiamele who gave his age as 10 years and 4 months, presented himself before Arago in Paris. He was himself a shepherd and the son of a shepherd of Sicily. It was early discovered that by methods peculiar to himself he resolved problems that seemed, at the first view, to require extended mathematical knowledge.

In the presence of members of the French Academy, Arago proposed the following questions:

What is the cubic root of 3,796,416? In about half a minute the child responded 156, which is correct.

One complicated problem ran: What number has the following peculiarity, that if its cube is added to five times its square, and from the result 42 times the number and 40 is subtracted, the remainder is nothing? Arago immediately repeated this question, and as, on the second time, he was saying the last word, the boy answered: "The number is 5."

Arago finally requested him to extract the tenth root of 282,475,249. Vito, in a very short time, found that the root is seven.

A brother and sister of Mangiamele were also noted calculators. A committee composed of Arago, Cauchy and others complained that "the masters of Mangiamele have always kept secret the methods of calculation that he made use of". It is not clear from this whether the masters knew, and refused to divulge the methods employed, or whether the boy himself was unable to enlighten them. He was quite uneducated.

F. W. H. Myers expressed the opinion that apparently Mangiamele lost his gift after childhood.

TRUMAN HENRY SAFFORD (1836–1901) (Bib. 2, 3, 4) was, like Zerah Colburn, the son of a Vermont farmer. Both his parents were former school teachers. The father had a strong interest in mathematics and the mother, we are told, was of an "exquisite nervous temperament". Young Safford showed a remarkable all-round precocity, similar to that of Ampère. In his third year "the grand bias of his mind was suspected". Later, his parents amused themselves "with his power of calculating numbers". When he was six years old, he was able to calculate mentally the number of barleycorns in 1040 rods (617,760) (see p. 79 for an explanation of the method). At the age of seven, he had "gone to the extent of the famous Zerah Colburn's powers".

About this time, he began to study books on algebra and geometry and, soon after, higher mathematics and astronomy. On his return from a short tour, in which he had been introduced to various scientific men, he set about constructing an almanac which was put to press when the author was just 9½ years old. In the following year he calculated four different almanac calendars. Whilst working on one of these he originated a new rule for obtaining moon-risings and settings, accompanied by a table which saved fully one-fourth of the time hitherto spent in casting moon-risings. This rule and the manuscript almanacs are preserved in the Harvard library, as are also new rules for calculating eclipses.

Chambers' Journal (Vol. VIII) relates how, at ten years of age, he was carefully examined by the Rev. H. W. Adams, with questions prepared beforehand. Adams says: "I had only to read the sum to him once. . . . Let this fact be remembered in connection with some of the long and blind sums I shall hereafter name, and see if it does not show his amazing power of conception and comprehension." The questions given him became continually harder. "What number is that which, being divided by the product of its digits, the quotient is 3; and if 18 be added, the digits will be inverted? He flew out of his chair, whirled around, rolled up his eyes and said in about a minute, 24." "What is the entire surface of a regular pyramid whose slant is 17 feet and the base a pentagon, of which each side is 33·5 feet? In about two minutes, after amplifying (sic) round the room, as his custom is, he replied 3354·5558." "How did you do it?" asked Adams. "Multiply 33·5 by 5" replied Safford, "and that product by 8·5 and add this product to the product obtained by squaring 33·5, and multiplying the square by the tubular area taken from the table corresponding to a pentagon." "Multiply in your head 365,365,365,365,365,365 by 365,365,365,365,365,365. He flew round the room like a top, pulled his pantaloons over the tops of his boots, bit his hands, rolled his eyes in their sockets, sometimes smiling and talking, and then seeming to be in an agony, until, in not more than one minute, said he, 133,491,850,208,566,925,016,658,299,941,583,225! . . . he began to multiply at the left hand and to bring out the answers from left to right." In the number of figures this exceeds Bidder's longest multiplication, but the repetition of the same figures simplifies this sum considerably.

On the invitation of the Harvard University, his father removed to Cambridge, U.S.A., and Safford was placed under the charge of Principal Everett and Professor Pierce. At the age of 14 he calculated the elliptic elements of the first comet of 1849. After graduating from Harvard in 1854, he spent several years there in the Observatory. He made many important astronomical calculations and discoveries and numerous contributions to astronomical journals.

Safford had a wide range of interests and an encyclopædic memory. Chemistry, botany, philosophy, geography and history, as well as mathematics and astronomy, were included in his field of study. After holding various positions, he became Professor of Astronomy in the Williams College in 1876, where he remained until his death in 1901.

Safford early outstripped Bidder in range of mental calculation, but with the aid of books, whereas Bidder's methods were entirely of his own discovery. He later acquired considerable skill in factorizing large numbers and seemed to be able to recognize, almost at a glance, what numbers were likely to divide by any given number, and remembering the divisors of any number he had once examined.

In 1845, Dr Dewey wrote of him: "He is a regular reasoner, on correct and established principles, taking the easiest and most direct course. As he had Hutton's *Mathematics*, and wanted some logarithms, his father told me that he computed the logarithms 1 to 60 by the formula given by Hutton. These were afterwards found to be the same in a table of logarithms, for the same number of decimals."

According to F. W. H. Myers, Safford's gift lasted only for about six years. His loss of power was remarkable in that his whole bent was mathematical. His boyish gift of calculation raised him into notice and he became a professor of astronomy. He had, therefore, every motive and every opportunity to retain the gift, if thought and practice could have retained it. Whereas, however, at ten years old he worked correctly in his head, in one minute, a multiplication sum whose answer consisted of 36 figures he was, some six or seven years later, neither more nor less capable of such calculation than his neighbours.

GEORGE PARKER BIDDER, Jr., Q.C. (*b.* 1837) (Bib. 2, 3), "the younger Bidder" was the eldest son of G. P. Bidder. It is stated that he possessed a remarkable visual memory; that he always saw mental pictures of figures and could conceive of no other possible way of doing mental arithmetic.

George Bidder, Jr. distinguished himself at Cambridge in mathematics, being seventh wrangler of his year. He later became a thriving barrister and Queen's Counsel. He considered the aids to mental calculation to be a powerful memory of a peculiar cast, in which the figures seemed to stereotype themselves without an effort, and an almost inconceivable rapidity of operation. The former gift, Bidder Jr. undoubtedly possessed in a high degree. The latter was congenital but developed, no doubt, by incessant practice and by the confidence thereby acquired.

Writing of his gift, Bidder Jr. said: "I myself can perform pretty extensive arithmetical operations mentally, but I cannot pretend to approach, even distantly, to the rapidity and accuracy with which my father worked. I have occasionally multiplied 15 figures by 15 figures in my head, but it takes me a long time and I am liable to occasional errors." Just before writing this, he tried the following to see if he could still do it:

"387,201,969,513,825 × 199,631,057,265,413.

I got in my head the answer

75,576,299,427,512,145,197,597,834,725

in which I think you will find four figures out of the 29 are wrong."

Mitchell was of the opinion that the younger Bidder's method of multiplying was, like Diamandi's, cross multiplication. Of his feats of calculation, and of the degree of his precocity in this field, we have little knowledge.

Bidder Jr. declared that his calculations "proceeded in a visible form" in his mind and that he could conceive no other possible way of doing mental arithmetic. It is said that he employed a mnemonic system, instead of natural memory, in remembering numbers and that he could play two games of chess, blindfolded, simultaneously.

According to the *Spectator* (1878, Vol. LI, p. 1634), the daughters of George Bidder Q.C. showed more than the average, but not extraordinary, powers of doing mental arithmetic. To test their calculating powers, Professor Elliott in 1877, asked them, "At what point in the scale do Fahrenheit's thermometer and the Centigrade show the same number at the same temperature?" The nature of the two scales had to be explained, but after that they were left to their own resources. The next morning, one of the younger girls (about ten years old) said it was at 40 degrees below zero. She had worked out the correct answer while in bed. Of a grand-daughter, who showed great visual memory, the statement is recorded: "When I hear anything remarkable read or said to me, I think I see it in print."

F. W. H. Myers (Bib. 4) questioned Bidder Jr. on the question of ambidexterity. He reports: "There was somewhat more of dextrocerebral capacity than in the mass of mankind." This, presumably, means that he was proficient with his left hand.

JACQUES INAUDI (1867–1950) (Bib. 3), an Italian by birth, passed his early years, like Mondeux. in tending sheep. His passion for figures began at the age of six, and at seven he could carry on mental multiplications of 5-figures by 5-figures. His education was very slight; he did not learn to read and write until he was 20 years old. Outside his mental calculations he had no special ability; his memory for most things, except figures, was rather poor and he was often absent-minded. He was a professional calculator, living by public exhibitions of his talent and for many years in retirement at Champigny in France. He demonstrated his gifts before large audiences in almost every capital in Europe and also in the United States.

Inaudi died on 26 November, 1950, at the age of 83. Obituary notices describe him as the author of *Curiosités Mathématiques* and *Mes Problèmes*. The Paris edition of the *New York Herald Tribune* of 28 November, 1950 states:

"M. Inaudi was a Piedmontese by birth and came to France as a shepherd boy. His extraordinary faculty for mental arithmetic soon attracted notice, and in 1892 he was presented to the French Academy of Sciences, which gave official recognition to his phenomenal performances. After that M. Inaudi travelled all over Europe and America demonstrating his mental powers. His most sensational performance was a match with three calculating machines set to work out three different arithmetical problems simultaneously. M. Inaudi always gave the answers before any of the three machines stopped ticking. Although the walls of his house were covered with testimonials from crowned heads, after court performances, M. Inaudi died in relative poverty. He had been living a retired life since 1934, but he continued to amuse his neighbours with his powers until the end of his life."

Naming the day of the week on which any given date falls was one of Inaudi's favourite problems. The reduction of years, months and days to seconds he accomplished almost immediately, knowing by heart the number of seconds for each of these periods. He solved by arithmetic, problems corresponding to algebraic equations of the first and, sometimes, of higher degree, also such problems as the resolution of a given 4- or 5-figure number into the sum of four squares. In these latter cases, however, he proceeded for the most part simply by trial aided, of course, by his skill in calculation and his familiarity with many squares, cubes, and higher powers.

The author had the privilege of conducting a number of tests with Inaudi. Considerable time was spent in the preparation of the problems before these were placed before him for his solution. They were all of the type given in this book but what was most impressive—even uncanny—was the promptitude of the responses. No blackboard was employed on this occasion and the answers were correct every time. When Inaudi was asked if he could give any indication of his methods all that he could say was that he "heard the answers". It was exactly as if he had known beforehand just what questions would be asked and had carefully worked out all the solutions.

At his regular performances, the programme included the subtraction of one 21-figure number from another; the addition of five 6-figure numbers, the squaring of 4-figure numbers; the division of one 4-figure number by another; the extraction of the cube root of a 9-figure number and the 5th root of a 12-figure number, or such similar problems as were proposed by members of the audience.

As each number was announced, he repeated it slowly to his assistant who then read it aloud, to make sure there was no mistake. Inaudi then repeated the number once more, after which he devoted himself to the solution of the problem, meanwhile making an occasional remark to keep the audience in good humour. Throughout the exhibition, he faced the audience, never once looking at the blackboard.

Actually, he began his calculation as soon as the number was given, and carried it on during the various repetitions of the numbers by himself and his assistant, so that by the time he seemed to begin the calculation he might be well advanced towards the solution. In this way he appeared to work much more rapidly than was actually the case.

Inaudi was a well-marked instance of the auditory memory type. When he thought of numbers, in calculations or otherwise, he did not see them in his "mind's eye". Numbers were for him primarily words which he heard as if spoken by his own voice and during his calculations he almost always pronounced at least some of these words, either with partial distinctness or in a confused murmur.

One of Inaudi's most powerful characteristics was his wonderful memory for figures. In one experiment, he was able to repeat, after a single hearing, though with an effort, 36 figures, read off to him slowly in groups of three, but in the attempt to repeat 50 figures under the same conditions he became confused and got only 42 of them right.

In an experiment made to determine in what time he could learn 100 figures, read off to him in groups as often as requested, he learned the first 36 in a minute and a half: the first 57 in four minutes: 75 in five and a half minutes and the whole 100 (actually, there were 105) in twelve minutes. On the other hand, he could repeat in order, at any time within a day or two, all the figures used in his last performance, whether in the statement of the problems, the answers, or in the intermediate calculations.

The number of these figures was, at times, as high as 300. The total duration of the performance was usually not more than ten or twelve minutes. Each new performance, however, blotted out of his memory, almost entirely, the figures used in the previous one; but such constants as the number of seconds in a year etc., as well as many powers and products and any particular numbers and results, in which for any reason he took a special interest, remained permanently with him.

These facts show how important it is to take account of the conditions of such experiments, if the figures established by them are to have scientific value. In an experiment lasting as long as one of his regular exhibitions, but under very different conditions, Inaudi could learn only a third of the number of figures he remembered with ease under his usual conditions. In these public performances, however, each number in the problem was repeated several times (once by the proposer of the question, once by the assistant and twice by Inaudi himself) and the figures of the various calculations and the results have a logical connection in the problem. Moreover, the numbers were learned in relatively short stages, separated by intervals in which they could be assimilated.

In Binet's experiments with Inaudi, the subject was given a written column of numbers, each of which was to be mentally increased or diminished; multiplied or divided, by the same number. In other words, the addend, subtrahend, multiplier or divisor was uniform for the whole given column of numbers. The results were called off down the column as fast as obtained, and the average time for each operation thus determined.

These tests were made on some of Binet's pupils, on Inaudi, and on four department store cashiers who were thoroughly practised in arithmetic. The account states that the cashiers could perform, mentally, 2-figure multiplications and in some cases, though with difficulty, 3-figure multiplications. The students were, of course, considerably slower than Inaudi and the cashiers; but the cashiers, in dealing with the smaller numbers to which they were accustomed, were quite as rapid as Inaudi and in some cases even slightly more rapid. In handling larger numbers, however, which exceeded the limits of their customary calculations, the inferiority of the four cashiers to Inaudi was very marked.

UGO ZANEBONI (*b*. 1867) (Bib. 3), an Italian, was born in the same year as his countryman, Inaudi, and received a fair education. He was described by F. W. H. Myers as "quick witted". Quoting from Italian sources, Mitchell states that his interest in numbers began at the age of 12, and when he was 14, it is claimed, he could solve any problems his teacher proposed to him.

While serving his term in the army he was for a time stationed at a railroad depot, where he amused himself by gradually committing to memory a vast body of statistics relating to time-tables, distances between different cities, populations, tariffs, etc. When he later took to the stage as a professional calculator, questions based on these statistics formed part of his regular programme. Among his usual feats were the repetition, either forwards or backwards, of a memorized number of 256 figures; the squaring of numbers up to four figures; finding the fifth power of two-figure numbers, and, conversely, extracting the fifth root of any number of ten figures or less, the cube root of any 9-figure number, and the square root of any number of 7 figures, or less, whether the given number was a perfect power or not.

In these problems, he was aided by his knowledge of many perfect squares, cubes, etc., as well as by various properties of two-figure endings, with which he was thoroughly familiar.

PERICLES DIAMANDI (*b*. 1868) (Bib. 3) was the son of a Greek grain merchant. He attributed his calculating gift to his mother who "had an excellent memory for all kind of things". One brother and one sister, out of a family of fourteen, shared his aptitude for mental arithmetic. He entered school at the age of 7 and remained there until he was 16, always standing at the head of the class in mathematics.

It was only after entering the grain business himself, in 1884, that he discovered his powers of mental calculation, which he now found very useful. He knew five languages—English, French, German, Roumanian, and his native Greek—and was a great reader. He read all he could find on the subject of mental calculation, and wrote novels and poetry. It will thus be seen that Diamandi's education was much better than Inaudi's and his range of interests correspondingly wider, but he was less precocious in calculation than his fellow-calculator. In his calculations, Diamandi was considerably slower than Inaudi, whether the numbers concerned were large or small.

It is stated that Diamandi had colour association for the names of various persons, the days of the week etc., and if a few figures in a given number differed in colour from the rest, he remembered the colours without effort. If the colour scheme were more complicated, however, he first memorized the number and then learned the colours of the individual figures. He always saw numbers as written in his own handwriting and preferably, if the numbers were large, in a rectangle as nearly square as possible, rather than in one or two long lines. He learned spoken figures (in French) much less rapidly than written since, in the case of spoken figures, not only was it necessary to call forth the corresponding visual images but also to translate the numbers into his native Greek, in which all his calculations were carried on. Where he endeavoured to learn the figures very accurately, for the purpose of calculation he was only about half as rapid as Inaudi but where he was concerned with speed rather than accuracy his times were much shorter. In the one case he learned 10 figures in 17 seconds; in the other, 11 figures in 3 seconds.

His time for a four-figure multiplication was 127 seconds, whereas Inaudi could accomplish the same feat in 21 seconds. Mitchell was of the opinion that Diamandi found the various figures of the product in order, from right to left, by cross-multiplication. Thus in such examples as

$$
\begin{array}{r}
46273 \\
729 \\
\hline
416457 \\
92546 \\
323911 \\
\hline
33733017
\end{array}
$$

he found the figures of the partial products, not in the horizontal lines of the ordinary method, but in vertical lines, first 7, then 5, 6: then 4, 4, 1; then 6, 5, 1; then 1, 2, 9; then 4, 9, 3; then 2; and, finally, 3. He added each column before he proceeded to find the numbers that composed the next column. This method has the advantage that the various figures of the partial products can be forgotten almost as fast as obtained, since that figure of the total product which depends on a given column of the partial product, is found and recorded as soon as the column is known. The numbers in that column, therefore, play no further part in the calculation.

It requires considerable practice to acquire this method of multiplication, especially to those trained in ordinary horizontal multiplication because the way of doing a thing to which one is accustomed becomes, in course of time, more or less automatic.

ARUMOGAM (b. 1896), a native of Ceylon, was described as "a live ready-reckoner" and was twelve years of age when his gift was first discovered. He was unintelligent and was unable to take care of himself or the money he earned through his exhibitions. He was fond of playing with marbles and it is stated that a gift of these gave him greater pleasure than a hundred rupees. No ancestors of talent could be traced.

Arumogam's only language was his mother tongue, Tamil, and it was necessary to explain his problems through an interpreter. His parents belonged to a section of the weaver caste, known in South India as the chalias, and were natives of Srivilliputtur, 46 miles from Marura. When her son was born, his mother called him after one of the names of the god "Arumukan", the "six-faced one". He had an extra finger on each hand and an extra toe on each foot and was similar to Colburn in that respect (*see p*. 25). As he grew up, it is stated, he spent his time at the sacred shrines begging for coppers and playing in the streets.

Arumogam's version of the origin of his gift is that at the great karkitai festival at Tirupparankunram, he had gone, as usual, to beg and worship. While he was sleeping at night, in the precincts of the temple, an ascetic (pandaram) appeared to him in a dream, and wrote something on his tongue, leaving a mark. Next morning when hanging around the shops in hope of charity, he remarked that the shopkeepers were dreadfully slow in making up their accounts, and that he could do their work far quicker. They tried him and found him extraordinarily gifted. Business firms employed him to straighten out complicated accounts.

The *Ceylon Morning Leader*, 7 September, 1912, gave a long account of certain tests imposed upon Arumogam. These were submitted to him at the monthly meeting of the Royal Asiatic Society, held at Colombo on 5 September, 1912. The President, Sir Hugh Clifford, Colonial Secretary, stated that the Education Department of Ceylon had spared no pains in setting a paper to puzzle Arumogam.

A representative of the Training College was present to explain the problems in Tamil. The questions were as follows:

Add together 8,596,497,713,826 and 96,268,593.

Multiply 1,001,001 by 100,100.

Multiply 45,989 by 864,726.

If 107 is multiplied by a certain number, it is increased by 2140. Find the multiplier.

Find the factors of (a) 28,413, (b) 89,712.

In a division sum, the divisor is twenty times the quotient and five times the remainder. What is the dividend if the remainder is 76?

If seventeen sovereigns form a column one inch high, how many would it take to represent a height of 3451 feet?

The diameter of a sovereign being seven-eighths of an inch, how many placed in contact would it require to stretch from London to Liverpool (196 miles)?

Find the square root of 63,409,369.

Find the cube root of 20,570,824.

Find the fifth root of 69, 343, 957.

Multiply (a) £84 17s. 6¼d. by 24: (b) £48 14s. 5¾d. by 7694.

A wheel has a circumference of 3¼ yards. How many times will the wheel turn in travelling 26 miles.

If a person sells 22 articles for the same money which he paid for 36, what does he gain per cent?

Find the simple interest on £584 for 42 days at five per cent.

At what rate per cent, simple interest, will a sum of money double itself in thirty years?

What weight of water is there in a room flooded two

inches deep, the room being 18 ft. 9 in. by 13 ft. 4 in. and a cubic foot of water weighing 62½ lb.?

A square field has a plantation eleven yards wide running along all four sides within the boundary of the field; this plantation contains one acre. Find the area of the field.

The record states that each of the above questions was correctly answered "in a few seconds" and that any slight delay that occurred was due to the necessity of interpretation.

The Chairman then requested a member of the audience to set a problem and a correct answer was given to the following in under three seconds:

A Chetty gave as a treat to 173 persons, a bushel of rice each. Each bushel contained 3,431,272 grains, and the Chetty stipulated that 17% should be given to the temple. How many grains did the temple get?

It is stated that Arumogam answered the questions put to him through rapid calculation by very short and original cuts. At the demonstration above referred to, a Mr. Arunachalam gave a description of his methods:

"Thus to take a simple sum of multiplication, say, of 2555 by 3437. Of course, he deals with figures in millions and billions, but I take this for simplicity of illustration. He would take the first number as 2500 (2½ thousand), the remainder being 55. The other number he would take as 3500 (3½ thousand), the difference being 63. He would multiply 2½ thousand by 3½ thousand, and then make the necessary addition for the remainder 55 and the necessary subtraction for the difference 63, and declare the result in the twinkling of an eye."

Arumogam was 16 years of age when the abovementioned demonstration took place. For some ten months subsequently a Brahmin hired him from his mother at 22 rupees a month and made large sums from his exhibitions. The boy was later placed in the care of a cashier of the Madras Bank.

EDWARD MILLS (*b.* 1902) was a native of Leeds. Before the First World War, Mills ran about the markets on weekdays and, on Saturday nights, was the magnet which drew crowds of people around a small stall where soap was sold. He would stand by the side of the stall and the proprietor would invite problems of calculation from the crowd. The author made some enquiries about Mills. In 1943, he was still alive, but very reticent with regard to his gift, a reference to which appeared in the *Leeds Mercury* in 1920.

In the markets he was known as "Datas" (so called after a famous music-hall artiste of those days, who specialized in memorizing dates). A Leeds man with theatre interests happened to hear Mills giving his answers with amazing quickness, with the result that eventually he became known as a stage star, both in this country and in America but, owing to his hatred of publicity, his career was not altogether a success.

Apparently, he was able to answer immediately such questions as: "You buy 15,497 articles at 1¾d. each: sell 7500 at 2½d. each and 7500 at 3¼d. The remainder were unsold. What profit would you make on the transaction?"

Mills could not explain how he arrived at his answers. He served in the Second World War and an effort was again made to get him to take to a stage career but this does not appear to have been successful.

MAURICE DAGBERT (*b.* 1913) (Bib. 16) was born at Calais, on 20 June, 1913. *Sciences Métapsychiques* (1947) has some interesting details concerning three extraordinary calculators and Dagbert is one of the three.

Dagbert had an ordinary primary school education and it is said that his knowledge of mathematics was practically nil. He left school when 12 years of age and at the age of 17 was brought into touch with Inaudi. His passion for figuring seems to date from that meeting. He made Inaudi his model and in order to emulate the feats of the master he devoted himself for a number of years to intensive training. This training was interrupted by the Second World War, in which he served and eventually spent some three years in a prison camp.

By 1945, his training had developed sufficiently to warrant his appearance before a commission at the French Academy of Sciences. It is said that his taste for calculation was very precocious, but we have no information concerning his earlier activities and he was nearly 32 years of age when he appeared before the Academy.

The report of the Academy was brief, but very favourable. It stated: "M. Dagbert's power of calculation appears to be comparable with that of Jacques Inaudi, who was presented before the Academy by Darboux in 1892. Like Inaudi, M. Dagbert is served by an excellent memory. He has stated that he combines the figures with the aid of extremely vivid images, which he obtained by closing his eyes or by fixing them on a white object (such as the ceiling of the room in which he is demonstrating). He sees the figures appear at the rate at which he hears them announced, as though he had written them on a board.

"One of the exercises carried out by M. Dagbert bears witness to this precise and durable faculty of recollection: it consists in the addition of six or ten numbers of six figures, which are dictated to him in sets of two figures, announced in any order, in such a way as to fill all the compartments of a board of three columns and six or ten lines. M. Dagbert, who has his back to the board, performs this feat as though he has the numbers in physical view."

During an exhibition, lasting some 2½ hours, Dagbert appears to have devoted a fair amount of his time to the demonstration of calendar problems. As an example of his arithmetical gifts, we are told that he extracted the cube root of 484,050,967,814,413 (= 78,517) in two minutes, and the fifth root of 50,260,731,820,489,949 (= 2189) in one minute and twenty-five seconds.

The report states that he visited Inaudi, when he was 14 years of age, but an article by M. de Cressac gives the year 1930 as the date of his visit to Inaudi, in which case he would be about 17 years old.

Dagbert told the Commission that he had taught himself the rules used in his calculations, which rules were for him "purely empirical and for which he is unable to give any reasons".

As a simple example, he told the Committee that to cube a number of two figures he made use of two key numbers, which he knew by heart but of which he could not give the origin.

The report concludes: "It is not surprising, under these conditions, that M. Dagbert, whose power and speed of calculation are remarkable in the domains with which he is well acquainted, should be baffled by very simple questions (such as one of the questions put to Inaudi when he was presented before the Academy in 1892), when these questions necessitated certain algebraic transformations."

After the session was over, M. Dagbert was introduced to the members of the Academy and carried out before them a few of the highly complicated mental calculations of which he was capable.

Fortunately, we are given by M. de Cressac many examples of the calculations usually carried out by Dagbert. We are told that the operations he usually performed were multiplications. The enormous additions or fantastic subtractions in which Inaudi excelled do not appear to have held his attention to any degree. As an example of his prodigious memory, we are told that he could give by heart the value of π to 707 places of decimals. As mentioned elsewhere (*p.* 149), Shanks, an English mathematician, in 1873, determined π to 707 decimal places. In the case of Dagbert, however, there was rather more to it than repeating, parrot-like, a long list. If he was asked to name the figure for, say, the 320th decimal place (or any other) it is claimed that he could give this accurately. Even assuming the use of mnemonics, this is no mean feat bearing in mind the length of the list that has to be covered.

In spite of this, Dagbert claimed that memory played no part in the "elaboration" of his answers. He stated that he had an infinite number of short-cuts which, says M. de Cressac "he used with a virtuosity that defies the imagination". He was able to give "instantaneous" answers to the following questions:

Multiply 3478 by 5685 (= 19,772,430)
Give the cube of 27 (= 19,683)
Give the fourth power of 34 (= 1,336,336)
Give the fifth power of 31 (= 28,629,151)
Give the sixth power of 72 (= 139,314,069,504)
Give the seventh power of 99 (= 93,206,534,790,699) etc.

In illustrating his methods, Dagbert stated that to multiply, say, 93 by 96 he would proceed on these lines. 93 from 100 leaves 7; 96 from 100 leaves 4. 7 × 4 = 28, which gives the last two figures. 93 minus 4 or 96 minus 7 gives 89, the resulting answer being 8928.

Dagbert gives other examples of his method of working, reference to which will be found in Chapter II.

To continue with the examples themselves, as an indication of his "prodigious speed" we are told that he

gave the cube root of 260,917,119 (= 639) in 4
gave the cube root of 14,886,936 (= 246) in 2
raised 29 to the sixth power (= 594,823,321) in 13
raised 89 to the sixth power (= 496,981,290,961) in 10
gave the cube root of 49,633,171,875 (= 3675) in 50
gave the number of seconds in 58 years (= 1,830,297,600) in 23.

(In giving the time occupied in working out the above examples, we are not told whether they are in minutes or seconds. It states that he did so and so "en 4" and another "en 2" and so on. Obviously, seconds are indicated.) Dagbert's last example, given above, is one of the few instances where a calculator has made due allowance for leap years.

M. de Cressac states that it seems, when making root extractions, M. Dagbert, actually carries out some kind of arithmetical process, but with an ability far beyond comprehension. We are told that Dagbert takes care "not only to call up numbers giving the root an exact figure, but also to get his interrogators to separate the numbers into sets of three figures, as though for an actual arithmetical process."

A departure from the usual methods was indicated when M. Dagbert was provided, at his request, with a violin. He then requested his audience to set him the task of extracting four cube roots, of three figures to the root, whilst he read, for the first time a simple piece of music. He undertook to give the results of his figuring at the end of 32 bars. We are informed that Dagbert did not claim to be a musician of any great ability. The piece selected was a little-known portion of a concerto by Albert Bachmann. He was asked to give the cube roots of 397,065,375: 57,960,603: 152,273,304 and 665,338,617. The four results asked for (= 735: 387: 534 and 873) were obtained, as forecast, in 1 minute 25 seconds.

M. de Cressac goes on to say: "All the calculations made by this performer are written in sequence on a blackboard. As soon as the board is full of figures, the subject repeats everything by heart and without error—but on one condition—the board thus prepared must always be perfectly clear and plain to his mental vision. If a figure is badly written: if a smudge of chalk has been incompletely rubbed out: if a sign has been added out of place, the whole marvellous mechanism of his memory falls to pieces. In fact, during the mnemonic process, the subject 'sees', so he tells us, the board with all its details and faults. If the figures have been well and clearly written, the recall is perfect but, otherwise, the contrary is the case."

The account does not state whether or not the performer himself wrote the figures on the blackboard but, in any case, it is difficult to understand why the figures had to be clear on the blackboard so as to be plain to his *mental* vision.

M. Dagbert considers this vision to be absolutely objective in character. Such a picture, properly assimilated, can, he tells us, be easily recovered later, at the will of the subject, even after considerable intervals of time. In this case it appears always in the form of an entirely objective vision and not in the form of habitual mental recollections.

As an example of Dagbert's amazing powers in the realm of numbers, we are told, that he will ask one person for a number of five figures, such as 53,799 and another for a six-figure number, such as 591,789. He then states that he will multiply the latter by 9091 and "by a miracle, the secret of which M. Dagbert alone knows", the public is surprised to see the result appear = 5,379,953,799. M. Dagbert carried out a considerable number of "recreations" of this kind, solely "by using the mechanism of his sub-consciousness". (*See p.* 88 for an explanation of this "miracle".)

M. de Cressac gives several examples of Dagbert's spontaneous replies to calendar questions. Dagbert adopts the unusual course of explaining the solution of these questions and gives, in detail, a method almost identical with that described later in this book (*p.* 185).

We are now given another of Dagbert's specialities. A blackboard is provided, on which are written the letters A, B, C and the numbers 1 to 7 as shown below, and members of the audience are invited to call out any two-figure numbers they care to select. For example, one would call B5, 35: another C7, 21 and so on, until eventually all the spaces on the board are filled. We are informed that during this performance Dagbert has his back to the board. He then repeats, by heart and without error, all the numbers that have been announced and in their normal sequence and makes the addition, figure by figure, without mistake. Finally, he repeats all the figures on the board just as though he had the board before his eyes.

	A	B	C
1	11	00	15
2	23	44	18
3	99	36	37
4	80	92	21
5	27	35	43
6	48	89	11
7	76	71	21

To conclude the performance, Dagbert gave a demonstration which will be of particular interest to those readers with a knowledge of mental magic: A person is asked to write, secretly, a number of three or four figures (such as 7809, for example). He is then asked to tell M. Dagbert the remainders after dividing this number by 17, 23 and 29 respectively. Assuming 7809 to be selected, the victim would tell Dagbert that 17 left a remainder of 6; 23 left a remainder of 12, and 29 a remainder of 8. These remainders would then be multiplied in turn by the numbers 8671, 3451 and 10557. The products are then added together, *i.e.*

$$6 \times 8671 = 52026$$
$$12 \times 3451 = 41412$$
$$8 \times 10557 = 84456$$
$$177894$$

The total (177894) is then divided by 11339. The remainder of the division will inevitably give the number originally, secretly, thought of, namely: 7809. The theory of this "secret" method is given in Appendix II.

SHAKUNTALA DEVI (*b.* 4 November, 1920). As this volume was nearing completion, there came to this country a young lady who was described in the Press as "The Human Comptometer". Miss Devi was born in a small village, near Bangalore. She is one of a family of six children and gave evidence of her calculating ability at the age of five. When only six years old, she was giving public exhibitions. A younger brother and sister have also given evidence of unusual calculating ability but to nothing like the same extent as their sister Shakuntala.

Early in October, 1950, soon after her arrival in this country, Miss Devi gave a demonstration of her powers in the "Picture Page" television programme. The demonstration included the usual "Day for any Date" so popular with mentalists and prodigies alike, but most of the short time available was devoted to the immediate extraction of square and cube roots from large numbers read out to her.

She specializes also in the mental multiplication of long numbers. Her root extractions go up to the seventh root. Her responses are immediate and it is claimed that in her public performances she had never been found wrong. Information from reliable sources indicates that at the age of seven at a demonstration in Bangalore "Her mental calculating powers were found to be remarkable, in that she could easily work out additions, subtractions, multiplications, divisions, square roots, G.C.M., L.C.M. of long and complicated figures". Concerning a demonstration at the age of nine, the Principal of H. H. The Maharaja's College writes: "She could easily manipulate figures up to ten digits in all the departments of mathematics such as cube root, square root, H.C.F., L.C.M., etc."

The author has interviewed Miss Devi and is hoping to have an opportunity of testing her remarkable powers. Various investigators claim that this young lady "sees the answers in her mind" but when questioned by the writer she was not at all sure about it. She stated that the answers "came" to her, but just how they came she could not explain. She is deeply religious and looks upon her calculating ability as a gift from God. She usually spends the twenty-four hours immediately preceding a demonstration in what she describes as "concentration". It would appear that the "concentration" consists of thinking, as far as possible, of nothing at all. She has a good knowledge of English and when asked questions in that language the replies come to her in her native dialect. There is no evidence of past members of her family possessing any exceptional arithmetical ability and in all other respects, physically and mentally, she appears quite normal.

Miss Devi anticipates spending some time in this country and in America and if a thorough investigation can be arranged it will possibly throw some light on these interesting problems.

OSCAR VERHAEGHE (*b.* 16 April, 1926) (Bib. 16) was born at Bousval, Belgium. The information in *Sciences Méta-psychiques* concerning this calculator was supplied by M. C. Fernand, ingénieur, or taken from the local press. Verhaeghe is referred to as "an adolescent of seventeen with the mental age of a babe of two years". From this description it will be obvious that we have here an instance of a person of feeble mind being able to work out intricate mental calculations. (A similar case is described on *p.* 73.)

We are told by M. de Cressac that very lengthy and most complicated arithmetical operations were performed, with amazing rapidity and without error, by a "deficient brain". The calculator can give no explanation of his gift, or is quite incapable of expressing himself about it. When questioned regarding his procedure he can only say, either that he does not know anything or that it simply comes to him.

At Uccle on 10 August, 1946, Verhaeghe was examined by a committee which included Mlle Pholien, of the Belgian Astronomical Society and MM. Moreau, Bourgeois, Arend, Roland, and Dof. Ladet, all of them well-known mathematicians. At a later sitting, held on 6 September, 1946, the mathematician Kraitchik, of the University of Brussels, was also present. Kraitchik is an eminent mathematician and the author of *Mathematical Recreations* (Bib. 17).

We are told that all the members of the committee were amazed at the accuracy of the results and the extraordinary rapidity of the replies.

Some of the questions answered by this calculator were as follows:

Multiply 4777 by 64 (= 305,728); 15 seconds.

Cube 689 (= 327,082,769); 6 seconds.

Give the fourth power of 1246 (= 2,410,305,930,256); 10 seconds.

Give the 59th power of 2 ($= 576,460,752,303,423,488$); 30 seconds.

Extract the sixth root of $24,137,585$ ($= 17$, remainder 16); 25 seconds.

Give the square of $888,888,888,888,888$ ($= 790,123,456,790,121,876,543,209,876,544$); 40 seconds.

Raise $9,999,999$ to the fifth power. (*Answer:* 35 figures) 60 seconds.

It is said that this young Belgian calculator, despite his great handicap, is physically by no means unattractive and of a jovial disposition. He is very timid, awkward, and somewhat fearful. His speech is very slow, jerky and confused. With the utmost docility, he lends himself to whatever tests are desired, however long they may be, except at meal times!

There is one curious paragraph in M. de Cressac's account, which is translated in full:

"Moreover, and this is a very important point, whereas M. Dagbert engages in a most ingenious and extraordinary intellectual feat for the purpose of preparing his replies, the process of which technique he has from time to time explained—and this, we repeat, seems both disconcerting and of extreme significance—M. O. Verhaeghe seems incapable of devising the slightest calculating artifice; the exact reply, through a badly defined mechanism, rises up in some way spontaneously to his mind."

MISCELLANEOUS

So that the list in this book may be as complete as possible, under this heading will be grouped a number of calculators concerning whom the author has been able to discover only very meagre details.

Scripture writes of a boy from St. Poelten who was exhibited by Gall in Vienna. He was the son of a blacksmith and had received no more instruction at school than his companions. At nine years of age, when they gave him three numbers, each expressed by ten or twelve figures, asking him to add them, then to subtract them two by two, to multiply and then divide them by numbers containing three figures, he would give one look at the numbers and announce the result before it could be obtained by others on paper.

Gall says that an advocate came to him to complain that his son, aged five years, was occupied exclusively with numbers and calculations, and that it was impossible to fix his attention on anything else.

Devaux, a boy of seven years, had a passion for going to all the fairs, and waiting for the traders at the moment when they had closed their accounts. When they made mistakes in their calculations, it was his greatest pleasure to discover the error.

Mr. Van R. of Utica, U.S.A., at the age of six years, distinguished himself by a singular facility for counting in his head. At eight, he lost this faculty, and after that time he could calculate neither better nor faster than any other person. He did not retain the slightest idea of the manner in which he performed his calculations in childhood.

Professor Elliott tells of a half idiot who was remarkable in his own country district for his powers of calculation. He got him to put down his operations in a few cases on paper; his modes of abbreviation were ingenious.

Mrs. F. E. Leaning, in an article on Calculating Boys (Bib. 11) writes: "The Mexican baby, Miguel Mantilla, at two years old began the same sort of calendar wonders that Fleury does. 'In what years did, or will, February 4th be a Friday?' asked Hyslop of him. Or 'What date was the second Sunday in 1840?' And all the answers were given in less than fifteen seconds."

Both Scripture and Mitchell (Bib. 2, 3) refer to a blind Swiss, mentioned by Johannes Huber, who not only solved the most difficult problems, but could repeat a series of 150 figures, either forwards or backwards, after a single hearing, or name at once, for example, the 80th or 30th figure from either end. Before becoming blind, he had been a man of very weak memory but, afterwards, busying himself with exercises in calculation, he discovered a very simple method of dealing with the largest numbers, and tried to sell his secret in England for a high price.

To round off this list in chronological order below will be found brief particulars of other minor prodigies:

Matthieu le Coq (*b.* about 1656), an Italian boy, at the age of six, without knowing how to read or write, was able to perform all the most difficult operations of arithmetic, such as the four elementary operations, the rule of three, square and cube root: and that too, as soon as the question was put to him. He learned to calculate by stringing beads.

John Mole (*b.* 1743) was a farm labourer of Ipswich. Taught only by his mother, Sarah, he rose to expert knowledge of algebra and of mental calculations by visualizing numbers. He eventually opened a school himself and published a number of works on mathematics.

Henry Andrews (*b.* 1743) likewise never went to school but became a schoolmaster and bookseller. At 10, he was observing stars and gave proof of his calculating ability. He calculated the eclipse of 1764 with exceptional accuracy. For more than 40 years, up to his death at Royston, he was a calculator for the *Nautical Almanack* and for Dr. Hatton of *Moore's Almanack*. He received both praise and a prize from the Board of Longitude.

George Watson (*b.* 1785) was born at Buxted in Sussex

and followed the occupation of a labourer. In everything but his extraordinary powers of memory and calculation, he was almost idiotic. Although unable to read or write he could, with facility, perform in his head the most difficult calculations. He also possessed the power of recollecting the events of every day, from an early period of his life. Upon being asked what day of the week a given day and month of the year occurred, he would immediately name it and, if it happened during his lifetime, he would mention where he was on that day and what was the state of the weather. His replies were invariably correct. He exhibited his powers in the neighbouring counties and in respect to his own county of Sussex could tell the number of churches, public houses etc., in every town, village and hamlet.

Richard Whateley (1778–1863) Archbishop of Dublin, was born in London on 1 February, 1778. He was a man of outstanding all-round ability. He began to calculate at the age of five but retained the power for only about three years. It was claimed that he probably surpassed Colburn but did not happen to hit on Colburn's favourite problem of extracting square and cube roots. His power left him when he started school and after that throughout his life as far as figures were concerned he was, to use his own language "a perfect dunce".

In the *Annual Register* 1788, appears an account of the career of a negro of Maryland who, with no education whatever, possessed a wonderful power for numbers and solved many difficult arithmetical questions that were put to him.

M. M. J. R. Lacy (*b*. 1795) was born in Bilbao, Spain. At a very early age he was exhibited in this country and created no small stir by his wonderful performances as a calculator.

A daughter of the Countess of Mansfield (*b*. about 1804)

was seen by Spurzheim in London, at the age of 13, at which time she "extracted with great facility the square and cube roots of numbers of nine places". Mitchell points out that whether this refers only to perfect squares and cubes is not clear. Colburn speaks of her as displaying in 1812, at the age of 8 or thereabouts a degree of mental quickness "uncommon in her sex and years". It is unfortunate that no details are available of what would appear to be one of the few girl calculators on record.

Vincenzo Succaro (*b.* 1822), a Sicilian, appeared in public as a calculator at the age of six. He received a good education but showed no special ability outside that of calculation.

Giuseppe Pugliese (*b.* "a little later" than Succaro) also a Sicilian, took to the stage at the age of five and gave calculating exhibitions in Italy and Germany. An attempt was made to teach him geometry but he was unable to deal with geometrical forms.

Grandmange (*b.* about 1836), who was without arms or legs, performed mentally very complicated calculations and solved difficult problems.

Prolongeau (*b.* about 1838), at the age of 6½ solved mentally with great facility, problems relating to the ordinary operations of arithmetic and was successful in the solution of equations of the first degree.

Dr. Ferrol (*b.* 1864) had a sister about one year his elder, who shared his gift for mental calculation. His father was an architect and a good reckoner. His mother's mind was occupied with architectural computations at the time of the birth of these two children. Whether this pre-natal influence had any effect on their mental powers cannot be determined. Ferrol's gift showed itself at an early age but as soon as he learned the elements of algebra, at the age of ten, he developed a preference for mental algebra over mental arithmetic. It is stated that he was the head of his class in arithmetic but below the average in all other subjects. He was a remarkably poor visualizer and his processes were "intuitive". The answer to a problem, he states, came instantly and was always correct. His general memory was about normal and his figure memory depended on mnemonics.

Luigi Pierini (*b.* 1878) learned late to speak and to walk, suffered from many children's diseases and was an epileptic. He tended sheep and thus learned to count. He developed a remarkable talent for mental arithmetic and, at an early age, became a professional calculator.

Louis Fleury (*b.* ?1907) was investigated by Dr. Osty and was referred to by Mrs. Leaning early in 1928 (Bib. 11). Fleury, it is claimed, is almost unique among the calculators in having been born blind. At the age of 15 he was so backward as to be relegated to a home for incurables. Whilst at this school for the blind, he managed the first three rules of arithmetic with difficulty but division was entirely beyond him and he was given up as hopeless. Osty compares him with such prodigies as Colburn and Bidder, but judging from the scant information available such a comparision does not seem feasible. It is claimed that he could divide a number like 5364 by 43 in four seconds and "when required to break up an equally high number into four perfect squares can respond correctly in 2 minutes 10 seconds". Fleury, Dr. Osty emphasizes, is remarkable in possessing a memory which can hold the previous result in a complicated calculation, while another process is being gone through, to obtain a final result. Fleury also specialized in the usual types of calendar questions.

P. Donym (Pseudonym, *b.* about 1910). Around the year 1922, the attention of the author was directed to a calculating boy, about twelve years of age, resident at a school for the feeble-minded in the Midlands. (*See p.* 66 for a similar case.) Donym was an imbecile and apparently hopeless, as regards learning, in every subject, except that of mental calculation. His gifts in the latter direction appear to have been on a par with that of other calculators, especially as regards a phenomenal memory for figures, and the ability to give immediate answers of long multiplication sums. The gift, in this instance, appears to have remained in force for a few years only.

A. S. Russell in *The Listener*, 11 July, 1934, refers to an account in *Nature* of an uneducated Arab boy who died in a Government asylum in Cairo. Although he was unable to read or write, this Arab boy possessed unusual arithmetical ability. He could square numbers of two digits almost immediately and could give the products and squares of numbers with three digits, within 8 to 43 seconds. He could extract the square roots of numbers with six digits very rapidly but cube roots took a little longer. He could break off in the middle of a calculation to attend to other matters and take up the reckoning again just where he had left off. His methods were not discovered but he had previously memorized the squares of all numbers with two digits. He was of low intelligence and died when he was 19 years of age.

The list of calculating boys included in this chapter, although formidable, is probably by no means complete. Full many a calculating genius may have been born and have died unknown to the world at large.

CHAPTER II

THE CALCULATIONS CONSIDERED

"What would life be without arithmetic, but a scene of horrors?" SYDNEY SMITH.

EVERY endeavour will be made in this chapter to keep, as strictly as possible, to an analysis of the problems handled by calculators, of which numerous instances appear in the preceding chapter, leaving to later pages a more general discussion of the main features that go to the mental make-up of a calculating prodigy.

To become a successful calculator, the first essential is a retentive memory for figures, far in excess of that possessed by the average individual. Memory, then, is a common factor in all cases. As a generalization, it may be said that calculating prodigies are born, not made. They possess an inherent natural gift for figuring which, in the case of the better-known prodigies at all events, cannot be equalled by the trained mentalist. On the other hand, much could be done by way of suitable training to produce a very good artificial copy of the natural product. It would be necessary for the would-be "prodigy" to begin at an early age and to concentrate, possibly for years, on short-cut arithmetical methods (of which there are thousands) and memory training in figures to the exclusion of other subjects. Whether the eventual results would be commensurate with the time and trouble involved is another question.

The fact must not be overlooked that, in the nature of things, a calculator soon becomes a specialist in his subject. He starts with marbles, pebbles, beads and such like. Eventually, his days are devoted to practice and demonstration and it becomes, with him, a whole-time occupation.

In evaluating the arithmetical activities of the prodigy who has reached this stage, it is important to keep in mind the question of repetition. The problems he is asked to solve are, in the main, similar in nature, if not in detail, to questions he has been asked hundreds of times previously. Thus, the resolution of the problems he is set is frequently more a question of memory than of actual calculating ability.

And now a word concerning the time taken by the calculator in answering the questions put to him. The usual method is this: members of the audience put the questions. The calculator may repeat the question immediately or include it in his answer. For example, the author asked Inaudi: "What day was 5 October, 1888?" His reply came immediately: "5 October, 1888 was a Friday." By repeating the question, he gained sufficient time to work out the answer.

Every calculator, whether natural or trained, makes his own short-cuts as he goes along. Some of these short-cuts belie their name but they have the immeasurable advantage that they soon become automatic with the result that the calculator may actually be unaware that he is using them. Here is an illustration; whilst writing this chapter, the author had occasion to multiply 48 × 21. The answer (1008) spontaneously came to mind. An immediate analysis of the mental process involved revealed the surprising information that both sets of figures had been reversed in the process of multiplying and the simpler course adopted of multiplying 84 × 12. This, in the instance mentioned, gives the same total and it would appear that whilst the process had not been consciously remembered it was subconsciously available when required.

Inaudi had on the stage with him a manager, who entered most questions on the blackboard, repeating the figures as he did so. This, of course, takes time, although he appeared to do it rapidly. If the calculator himself writes the question on the blackboard, it also gives him time and helps considerably in memorizing. If the question on the blackboard is visible to the calculator, it is an additional help.

To the mentalist, mnemonic crutches are of much assistance in memorizing figures. Some of the calculators also frankly admitted that they used such artificial aids and it is quite likely that others used them without realizing that they were doing so.

CALENDAR PROBLEMS

Many of the results that have gained acclamation for the calculator are to problems that an experienced mentalist would take in his stride, *e.g.* calendar problems. Almost every calculator of note, has included in his demonstration evidence of his ability to name immediately the day of the week upon which any specified date may fall. Inaudi was in his element when dealing with this type of question and called out the answers as rapidly as members of the audience put their questions to him. In this case, it was not usual for either the questions or the replies to be written on the blackboard.

This calendar business, to the uninitiated, sounds impressive and that probably accounts for its popularity, but the routine is so simple as to be known to every mental magician. It calls for no feats of memorizing and a little practice will enable any person of average intelligence to emulate Inaudi. The procedure will be found in the chapter on *Arithmetical Problems* (*see p.* 183).

Another typical problem, associated with time, is for the calculator to name the number of minutes, or seconds, in a given period. In many instances the replies given by the calculators were inaccurate, because no allowance had been made for leap years. It is one of the simplest questions to answer. Most calculators would know by heart the number of seconds in a week, month and year. The figure 8 in connection with hundreds and thousands, plays a prominent part in British measures and "weeks to minutes" resolves itself into multiplying by eight, as will be seen later (*p.* 207).

SQUARING, CUBING AND MULTIPLICATION

Arithmetical processes to the inexperienced are matters of wonder, and the larger the numbers involved, the greater their amazement. This particularly applies to the squaring and cubing of numbers, many examples of which appear in the sums set to calculators. In the portion of this book on squaring and cubing, will be found various suggestions and methods of dealing with this kind of calculation (*see* Chap. XIV). From these examples, it will be clear, that squaring and cubing do not present any serious difficulties to the would-be mentalist. As an example of this reference is made elsewhere (*p.* 188) to A. H. Russell's book on *Rapid Calculations* (Bib. 12). Russell claims that to square a five-figure number should not take more than thirty seconds and for a seven-figure number, the mentalist is allowed just twice as long, *i.e.* one minute. These times, compare favourably with those occupied by professional calculators for similar problems.

It will be obvious that in all cases of squaring, cubing and multiplication generally, it is a tremendous advantage to be able to multiply any two 2-figure numbers together. Most ordinary people however, have little use for these extended multiplication tables. It takes a long time to learn them and a very short time to unlearn them. Practice, however, makes for perfection and, by constant use, they become automatic. An examination of the questions put to calculators will show that they are frequently asked to mention the square or the cube of any given numbers. This type of question also presents no serious difficulty to the mentalist, as will be indicated later (Chap. XIV). Similar remarks apply to multiplications of all types and the reader may want to know why, if this is so, these simplified methods are not taught in the schools? The answer is that many of them could, with considerable advantage, be popularized but the departures from standard practice would be so numerous as to preclude this because of the time taken.

An interesting feature connected with multiplication is that some of the more intelligent prodigies, such as Colburn and Bidder, were in the habit of multiplying from left to right, instead of vice-versa, as in the usual method. They claimed that by such means the larger numbers, with all their zeros, could be more easily remembered and the problem could be worked a step at a time. Thus, each fresh step incorporated the previous steps, which could be forgotten, with the result that the strain of memorizing was not so great. In explaining why beginning at the left was easier and necessary, Bidder states: "I could neither remember the figures (in the ordinary way of multiplying), nor could I, unless by a great effort, on a particular occasion, recollect a series of lines of figures; but in mental arithmetic you begin at the left-hand extremity, and you conclude at the unit, allowing only one fact to be impressed on the mind at a time. You modify that fact every instant as the process goes on; but still the object is to have one fact and one fact only, stored away at one time." In working the example 373 × 279 "I multiply 200 by 300 = 60,000: then multiplying 200 by 70, gives 14,000. I then add them together, and obliterating the previous figures from my mind, carry forward 74,000 etc. The last result in each operation, alone, is registered by the memory, all the previous results being consecutively obliterated until a total product is obtained."

Various other little helps were used. Bidder reveals some

of them, *e.g.* "in questions involving division of time, distance, weight, money etc., it is convenient to bear in mind the number of seconds in a year, inches or barley-corns in a mile, ounces and pounds in a hundredweight, and ton, pence and farthings in a pound sterling, etc. These are always ready for use when they could be applied with advantage. Suppose it is required to find the number of barley-corns in 587 miles—the ordinary processes, viz: 1760 × 587 × 3 × 12 × 3 = 111,576,960, when worked out, required 56 figures, while, mentally, I should multiply the number of barley-corns in a mile (190,080) by 587."

To get back again to an examination of the results; it is interesting to learn that Safford, at the age of six, was able to multiply mentally the number of barley-corns in 1040 rods. There are 594 barley-corns in a rod. It is easy mentally to multiply 1040 by 6 = 6240. He would add two noughts for the 600, giving 624,000 and as this is too great he would deduct 6240 from 624,000 giving the answer 617,760. Some of these examples are so elementary as to be hardly worth recording.

The problem (*see p.* 23) answered by Colburn in ten seconds on the number of steps taken in going from Concord to Boston reduces itself to finding the number of yards in 65 miles. Every schoolboy knows (or should do!) that there are 1760 yards in a mile, so all that Colburn had to do was to multiply 1760 by 65. A prodigy should have answered this at once!

Lucas, a French mathematician, writing in 1884 said: "I formerly knew an instructor whose scholars, of eight to twelve years of age, for the most part knew the multiplication tables extended to 100 by 100 and who calculated rapidly in the head the product of two numbers of four figures, in making the multiplication by periods of two figures."

What have the calculators to tell us concerning their

methods of working? Very little that is really helpful but still sufficient to indicate, in many instances, the crudity of the steps they employ. Many of them claim that they have not the slightest idea how it is done—the answer just comes visually into their minds, or they hear it mentally.

Mitchell suggests that, as stated on *p.* 17, the slowness of Buxton's calculations clearly indicates that his methods were those of counting rather than of multiplication. Dare the author say that there is not a great deal of difference between the two? Multiplication resolves itself into continuous addition and division into continuous subtraction. Primitive man could not distinguish between multiplication and addition and the primitive methods adopted by an illiterate calculator may have some connection with those adopted by his forbears.

When giving the square of 999,999 (*p.* 26), Zerah Colburn observed that he obtained the result by multiplying the square of 37,037 by the square of 27. To give an immediate answer (999,998,000,001) a modern magician would adopt a much shorter method (*see p.* 248). It is doubtful whether this would be more rapid, however, since, as already suggested, use becomes second nature in calculations, as in many other things.

There appears to be more reason in Arumogam's methods than in those of most of his fellow-calculators. One example has been quoted (*p.* 56), that to multiply 2555 by 3437, he would take $2\frac{1}{2}$ times $3\frac{1}{2}$ (2500 × 3500), and make the necessary addition and subtraction. This, although not so simple as the methods indicated later in this book, does show that a certain amount of common-sense was brought to bear on the problem.

Reference has already been made to the use of extended multiplication tables. In the case of Bidder, R. A. Proctor suggests it might reach to 1000 by 1000 although Scripture suggests only up to 100 by 100. In view of what Bidder himself has to say concerning his powers, it is very improbable that the whole of the tables were memorized. The results, in most instances, were obtained with such incredible rapidity as to give the impression that extended multiplication tables had been used.

As mentioned earlier, Colburn was once asked: How many times would a coach wheel, 12 ft. in circumference, turn round in 256 miles. There are 1760 yards in a mile and the wheel was 4 yards in circumference. In one mile it made 440 revolutions and in 256 miles it made

$$256 \times 440 = 112,640.$$

These very short examples indicate that, when you get down to it, what may appear to be intricate problems are often extremely simple to solve.

BIDDER'S METHODS

Bidder who, mainly by his own efforts, rose from obscurity to become one of the most successful and educated men of his time, went the same way about his problems as would a modern mentalist. In a paper read before the Institution of Civil Engineers, in February, 1856, with Robert Stephenson in the chair, he said: "Mental arithmetic can be done as easily, if not with greater facility than ordinary arithmetic. Undoubtedly the acquirement has ended in raising me from the position of a common labourer, in which I was born, to that of being able to address you as one of the Vice-Presidents of this distinguished Society. . . . If I am asked the product of, say, 89 by 73, the answer (6497) comes immediately into my mind. I multiply 80 by 70, 80 by 3, 9 by 70 and 9 by 3."

It will be seen that this operation is simply a question of memorizing the figures. If a blackboard is used and the question visible to the calculator, it helps considerably. In his days as a mentalist, the author adopted a simplified method of multiplication. By reference to the chapter on *Lightning Calculations* (*p.* 206) it will be seen to be the same as Bidder's procedure, described above. It required considerable practice to retain the question in the memory but that was the only difficulty. On attempting to repeat the performance, some twenty years later, it was found to be hopeless, through the practice not having been kept up.

In his famous article (Bib. 6) Bidder says: "In order to multiply up to three places of figures by three figures, the number of facts I had to store in my mind was less than what was requisite for the acquisition of the common multiplication table up to 12 times 12. For the latter, it is necessary to retain 72 facts; whereas, my multiplication up to 10 times 10 required only 50 facts. Then I had to recollect, in addition, the permutations among the numbers up to a million; that is to say, I had to recollect that 100 times 100 were 10,000; 10 times 10,000 were 100,000 and that ten hundred thousands made a million. . . . Therefore, all the machinery requisite to multiply up to three places of figures was restricted to 68 facts. If you ask a boy abruptly 'What is 900 times 80?' he hesitates and cannot answer, because the permutations are not apparent to him; but if he has the acquired facts as much at his command as he had any fact in the ordinary multiplication table, viz, that 10 times 10 equals 100 and 900 times 80 was nothing more than 9 times 8 by 100 times 10, he would answer off-hand 72,000; and if he could answer that he could easily say, 900 times 800 = 720,000. If the facts were stored away in his mind so as to be available at the instant he would give the answer without hesitation. If a boy had that power at his command he might at once, with an ordinary memory, proceed to compute and calculate three places of figures."

The following gives an insight into the rapidity of Bidder's associations: "Suppose I had to multiply 89 by 73:

I should say instantly 6497. If I read the figures written out before me I could not express a result more correctly or more rapidly. This facility has, however, tended to deceive me, for I fancied that I possessed a multiplication table up to 100 times 100, and when in full practice even beyond that; but I was in error. The fact is that I go through the entire operation of the computation in that short interval of time which it takes me to announce the result. . . . The velocity of the mental processes cannot be adequately expressed; the utterance of words cannot equal it. . . . Were my powers of registration at all equal to the powers of reasoning or execution, I should have no difficulty, in an inconceivably short space of time, in composing a voluminous table of logarithms."

COLBURN'S METHODS

The least intelligible of all the explanations given was that by Colburn. His friends tried to elicit a disclosure of the methods by which he performed his calculations, but for nearly three years he was unable to satisfy their enquiries. He positively declared that he did not know how the answers came into his mind. In London he made a couple of explanations. In one case, where he was asked to tell the square of 4395; he at first hesitated . . . but when he applied himself to it he said it was 19,316,025. On being questioned as to the cause of his hesitation, he replied that he did not like to multiply four figures by four figures; "but," said he, "I found out another way. I multiplied 293 by 293, and then multiplied this product by the number 15, and again by 15, which produced the same result". On another occasion, when asked the product of 21,734 multiplied by 543, he immediately replied 11,801,562. Upon some remark being made on the subject, the child said that he had, in his own mind, multiplied 65,202 by 181, *i.e.* he divided the smaller number (543) by 3 and multiplied the larger number by the same amount. This is a very useful hint. For example, if the mentalist is asked to multiply 812 by 36 it is easy mentally to convert this into 2436 × 12.

In an appendix to his *Memoir*, Colburn attempts to explain his methods of finding square and cube roots. His rule, first formulated two years after he began, was so clumsy and involved as to be of little help and he admitted that it was "a drag of a method".

SOME REMARKS ON PRECOCITY

Frank D. Mitchell, who was a pioneer in the study of calculating boys, and to whose views importance must be attached, is very insistent in his statements that there is nothing wonderful or incredible in this gift. He writes (Bib. 3): "Neither mathematical nor general education nor mental ability has any *direct* influence on mental calculation. Indirectly, however, education may have an important influence. We have seen that if, for any reason, the interest in calculation is lost, the calculating power will disappear. Now mental calculation is a narrow and special field, with little practical importance for most men; hence, other things being equal, as a boy's sphere of interests widens, his interest in mental calculation is likely to sink into the background. This explains why so many ignorant men have excelled as calculators; ignorance, by preventing the intrusion of other interests, leaves the calculator free to develop his one gift, and keeps him from realizing how trivial it is, and how groundless is the public amazement which, perhaps, contributes to his support.

"Given a knowledge of how to count, and later, a few definitions, as in Bidder's case, and any child of average mental ability can go on, once his interest is aroused, and construct unaided practically the whole science of arithmetic; no matter how much or how little he knows of other things. . . . Once the elementary processes are mastered, such operations as the reduction of years to seconds, compound interest, and any other arithmetical problems, are simply a matter of understanding the meaning of the question and then applying known rules, plus a varying amount of ingenuity, to the solution.

"We must note, furthermore, that practically an unlimited amount of time may be available for these calculations, if the prodigy wishes so to use it. Mental arithmetic requires no instruments, or apparatus; no audible practice that might disturb other members of the family: no information, save such chance scraps as may be picked up almost anywhere for the asking, or absorbed, without even the trouble of asking questions, from older brothers and sisters as they discuss their school lessons. The young calculator can carry on his researches . . . at almost any time during the twelve or fourteen hours of his waking day, except when he is engaged in conversation or active play. . . . These considerations put the whole matter of mathematical precocity in a new light. Instead of joining in the popular admiration and awe of these youthful calculators, we must say that precocity in calculation is one of the most natural things in the world. If a person is to become a calculator at all, he will usually begin as soon as he learns to count, and in most cases before he learns to read or write."

It would be unfortunate if the above remarks, and others in a similar strain in this book, should give the reader the impression that we are wasting our time in studying the activities of these calculating boys. The contrary is the case—we have here a faculty which, in the past, has never been thoroughly explored. The subject bristles with interest and, conjointly with the study of allied phenomena, may lead to discoveries which may have a tremendous bearing on our knowledge of the mind and its workings.

We turn now to the article in *Sciences Metapyschiques* (Bib. 16) regarding Inaudi, Dagbert and Verhaeghe.

There is no fresh information concerning Inaudi, and there is little to add regarding Verhaeghe. His gift is similar to that of the feeble-minded boy in the Midlands (*see p. 73*). The arithmetical problems set Verhaeghe would not bother a magician, provided he was not asked to perform these operations mentally. Therein, of course, lies the difference. Mentally, to square a number of fifteen figures, involving a reply of thirty figures, in a period of forty seconds, is an amazing feat which not one in a hundred millions could undertake successfully. It would almost appear that the mental infirmity of the calculator is a help, instead of a hindrance. This certainly appears to be an instance of the subconscious mind being given every opportunity for free expression, without let or hindrance on the part of the conscious mind.

DAGBERT'S METHODS

Many significant features are to be found in the information we are given concerning M. Dagbert. There is every evidence to show that Dagbert is a clever arithmetician, with a knowledge of the subtleties and dodges of a capable magician. He is not a prodigy in the accepted sense of the term. He is the example we have been seeking of what can be done by someone with a natural gift for figures who is prepared to devote a considerable amount of time to the development of the technique of a mentalist. The nature of his replies and descriptions of his methods of working reveal the skill of the magician and go to prove that a knowledge of figures, plus a knowledge of legerdemain, plus the time available for development will enable a suitable trainee to compete with the prodigies on their own ground. What better method could there be of combating the monotony of a prison camp than that of concentrating on mental arithmetic?

We are told that at the Academy of Sciences Dagbert was baffled by very simple questions but, unfortunately, we are given no indication of the nature of those questions. Some of the miracles he performed were "magic" pure and simple. M. de Cressac makes mention of Dagbert's extraordinary intellectual gymnastic feats for the purpose of preparing his replies. There are numerous instances where this was most obvious, *i.e.* in giving a cyclic number.

We are also informed that "the enormous additions and fantastic subtractions, in which Inaudi excelled, do not appear to occupy his attention to any degree". An explanation, of course, is that addition and subtraction do not lend themselves to conjuring, as do multiplication and division.

It is freely admitted that Dagbert made use of mnemonics and there is strong evidence in support of this in the blackboard demonstrations he gave before the Academy of Sciences and elsewhere. There is nothing more wonderful about this than about the similar performances of many magicians. At one time, when mental magic was in favour, this type of blackboard demonstration was one of the stock exhibitions. It is said that Dagbert was precocious but no evidence is given in support of this statement in the articles referred to.

It is not, for a moment, suggested that Dagbert is a fraud, or that he is claiming to be something that he is not. On the contrary, he was unusually helpful on many occasions by explaining his methods. He gives a good performance, so why should we question his own assurance that he has "an infinite number of calculating tricks"?

It is possible that the arithmetical reader will have spotted Dagbert's "secret", described by M. de Cressac as "a miracle—solved by using the mechanism of his sub-consciousness" (*see p.* 63). It will be recalled that Dagbert asked one person for a number of five figures, such as 53,799 and another person for a six-figure number "such as 591,789". It does not say that this second number was "forced". This, no doubt, passed unnoticed but when this had been done all was plain sailing. In effect, Dagbert simply multiplied 53,799 by 100,001. So that it would not be too conspicuous, however, the multiplication was conducted in two parts—first by 11 and then by 9091.

By way of explaining let us illustrate this with a smaller number, say, 261. Suppose then that 261 is the first number called. The mentalist next asks someone else for a four-figure number. Suppose this to be, say, 8423. Now 2871 (that is, 261 × 11) is wanted for the second number, and so the next step would be to ask the person who gave 8423 to deduct 5552 from this. This would give the required number of 2871, which when multipied by 91 results in the cyclic number 261,261.

CHAPTER III

THE EVOLUTION OF COUNTING

As yet a child, nor yet a fool to fame,
I lisped in numbers, for the numbers came.

ALEXANDER POPE.

THE earliest proof of arithmetical knowledge goes back to some 2150 years B.C. This proof is derived from two tablets found in 1854 at Senkerch, on the Euphrates, by the British geologist, W. K. Loftus. These tablets contained the squares of all numbers from 1 to 60 and the cubes of all numbers from 1 to 32. Soon after the discovery of the Senkerch tablets, a large number of tablets came to light at Nippur, an ancient city lying to the south of Babylon, and among these are many that relate to arithmetical problems.

There is little doubt that the ten Arabic figures: 1, 2, 3, 4, 5, 6, 7, 8, 9, 0, took their origin from the ten fingers of the hands. Fingers were used before figures and are still employed for counting by savage and by sage. It is a far cry from five-finger exercises to the results obtained by arithmetical prodigies but the connection between the two may be closer than is realized.

Although there are various opinions respecting the early use of these numerals, the one most generally accepted is that they were brought into Europe from Spain; that the Spaniards received them from the Moors; the Moors from the Arabians and Arabians from the Indians.

It is observed by Huet as a remarkable circumstance that for calculation and numerical increase the number 10 is always used, and that decimal progression is preferred to every other. The cause of this preference, of course, arises from the number of our fingers, upon which men accustom themselves to reckon from their infancy.

The number 10 is not so convenient and useful a number as 12. Ten can only be divided by two and five, but twelve can be divided by two, three, four and six. Many unlettered people cannot count beyond ten and some cannot even reckon beyond five. Plutarch says that decimal progression was used not only among the Greeks, but also by every uncivilized nation. Despite the fact that at least two of the calculators (Colburn and Arumogam) had six fingers on each hand and six toes on each foot, there is no evidence to indicate that they were acquainted with the advantages of duodecimals—proceeding in computation by twelves.

We have become so accustomed to the employment of decimal notation that most people do not look upon it as the mathematical device that it really is. Had we all been born with the extra digits possessed by these two calculators, the duodecimal scale would, undoubtedly, have become universally used and this, in the opinion of many, to the advantage of all concerned.

ROMAN NUMERALS

The learned authors of the *Nouveau Traite Diplomatique* have given some curious notices of the origin of the Roman numerals; thus to mark the first four numbers they used I's, which naturally represent the four fingers. To mark the fifth, they chose a V, which is made by bending inwards the three middle fingers, and stretching out only the thumb and the little finger; and for the tenth they used an X, which is a double V—one placed under the other. From this the progression of these numbers is always from one to five, and from five to ten. The hundred was signified by the capital letter of that word in latin = C-entum. The other letters, D for 500 and M for 1000 were afterwards added.

They frequently abbreviated their characters, by placing

one of these figures before another; and the figure of less value before a higher number denotes that so much must be deducted from the greater number. For instance, IV signifies five less one (*i.e.* 4); IX = ten less one (*i.e.* 9); but these abbreviations are not found amongst the ancient monuments. On clock and watch faces, when the hours are given in Roman numerals, we observe that four is shown IIII. It was altered in deference to the whim of one of the kings of France (Charles V) and has remained in this form ever since. (For list of Roman numerals *see* Appendix IV, *p.* 249.)

That men originally counted by their fingers is no mere supposition; it is still practised naturally by many. In semi-civilized states, small stones have been used, and the etymologists derive the words "calculate" and "calculations" from calculus, the Latin term for a pebble and by which they denominated their counters used for arithmetical computations

Many of the calculators began their arithmetical career by playing with pebbles. With 10 or 20 stones as counters, scores of arithmetical combinations are possible in the way of adding, subtracting, multiplying and dividing. One little pile of 5 stones added to another similar pile would give ocular and tactile proof that 5 + 5 makes 10 and that 5 × 2 also makes 10. Similarly, by taking 5 stones from a pile of 10 stones, the youthful calculator would soon discover that 10 — 5 or 10 divided by 2 = 5.

Madame Montessori, one of the pioneers of modern education, based her methods of teaching on the tactile sense. Wooden letters and figures are placed in the hands of the child so that a concrete image of each is formed by touch. In this way, the mental picture of the letters and figures is established much more rapidly than by the old methods of first learning to write. The child who has 5 marbles and acquires another 5 has a practical demonstration that

5 + 5 are 10 which is of far greater educational value than merely memorizing that 5 times 2 are 10.

CHINESE COUNTING

Nearly a century ago, reference was made by Sir J. Bowring, who was said to have a competent knowledge of a hundred languages, to the ingenious application in China of the fingers for the use of all sums whether of addition, subtraction, multiplication and division from one up to a hundred thousand.

In this ancient Chinese system, every finger on the left hand represents nine figures; the little finger the units, the ring finger the tens, the middle finger the hundreds, the forefinger the thousands, the thumb the tens of thousands. The three inner joints represent from 1 to 3, the three outer 4 to 6, the right side 7 to 9. The forefinger of the right hand is used for pointing to the figure to be called into use; thus, 1034 would at once be denoted by just touching the inside of the upper joint of the forefinger, representing 1000; then the inside of the second, or middle, joint of the ring finger, representing 30; and, lastly, the upper joint of the little finger touched on the outside, representing 4. Again, 99,999 would be represented by touching the side of the lower joint of the thumb (90,000) and the lower side of the joint of the fore, middle, ring, and little fingers, representing respectively 9000, 900, 90 and 9. The accuracy of accountancy in China and the rapidity with which all trading and commercial accounts are calculated, are matters of fact to all who have any acquaintance of accountancy in that country.

CALCULATING MACHINES

In the East, the use of the fingers, however, has been largely superseded by the more convenient abacus, or bead frame, which is almost universally used. In fact, it is claimed that in Asia, at the present day, more people use the abacus for accounting than use pencil and paper. American periodicals in November, 1946, gave considerable publicity to a series of comparative tests between the abacus and a modern desk calculating machine. Kiyoshi Mastuzaki, a clerk in the Japanese communications department, using the abacus challenged Private Thomas Wood, an expert calculating machine operator, using a modern calculator and defeated him in a speed and accuracy contest involving additions, subtractions, multiplications and divisions. On the other hand, there is no comparison between the time it takes to train an abacus expert and the rapidity with which an operator can become proficient with the more modern machine. The abacus was the first mechanical calculating machine to be put to practical use. It is believed to have been invented about 2600 B.C. It was adopted in very early times in India from where its use spread westward to Europe and eastward to China. It was, however, not in common use in Europe until towards the end of the thirteenth century.

It appears unlikely that any of the calculators mentioned in this book made use of the abacus but the principles involved here are not altogether dissimilar to those employed in playing with pebbles. In the East, where the abacus has been popular for centuries, most complicated arithmetical operations can be performed with this simple device, by persons entirely illiterate.

Until comparatively recent times what was known as the score or tally was widely employed in this country. This sense of the word arose from the habit of giving the two parties to a bargain each a cut stick, on which the amount at issue between them was duly recorded by means of notches. As these sticks corresponded, or ought exactly to correspond, with one another, a tally came to be popularly thought of as necessarily implying correspondence. In the English exchequer such strips of notched wood were given as receipts as late as the end of the eighteenth century, but at last they were accompanied by a written discharge as well, and only remained as a pure ceremonial and administrative survival. (*See* Appendix I, *p.* 245.)

The first real aid to calculation, in the British Isles, was the introduction in 1617 by the famous John Napier of Merchiston (the inventor of logarithms), of what came to be known as Napier's rods, or Napier's bones. Many specimens of these rods and their subsequent developments are to be found in the Science Museum, South Kensington. They were used to facilitate the multiplication and division of large numbers and usually consisted of some ten or twelve strips, about six inches in length, containing on each side a double series of numbers. They were not only popular but also "fashionable" and were of real value where long and laborious calculations were involved.

Blaise Pascal, in 1642, was the first to introduce the forerunner of the modern calculating machine. Its operations were confined to addition and subtraction. A machine invented by Morland, an Englishman, followed some twenty years later and from then onwards other makes, embracing substantial improvements, were introduced from time to time. It is not possible to give in this book even a brief description of the wonderful electrically operated machines now available for calculating, tabulating and accounting as they are far too numerous to enumerate.

A modern mathematician is far more favourably placed than his predecessor, of even a century ago, in that involved calculations which formerly occupied many days can now be conducted in almost as many minutes. It is partly due to the degree of perfection attained in these machines that the application of mathematics to practically every branch of science has increased to an almost incredible extent.

Time was when a good mathematician must of necessity be a good arithmetician but to be "quick at figures" is not essential in this modern age.

In considering the functions of calculating boys we should be careful to distinguish between arithmetic and mathematics. These boys have often been described as "mathematical prodigies" which, with few exceptions, they were not. They were arithmeticians, pure and simple— often with the emphasis on "simple".

The term "mathematics" was originally the collective name for geometry, arithmetic and certain physical sciences (such as astronomy and optics) involving geometrical reasoning. In modern use it is applied, in a strict sense, to the abstract science which investigates deductively the conclusions implicit in the elementary conceptions of spatial and numerical relations, and which includes as its main divisions geometry, arithmetic, and algebra. In a wider sense, it includes those branches of physical or other research which consist in the application of this abstract science to concrete data. When the word is used in this wider sense, the abstract science is distinguished as pure mathematics, and its concrete applications (*e.g.* in astronomy, physics, etc.), as applied or mixed mathematics.

In pointing out the association between a calculating boy and a modern mathematician we should perhaps remind the reader of the tremendous importance, at the present day, of the science of mathematics. Unfortunately, it seems to have played as great a part in the destruction of life as it has in increasing its amenities but pure knowledge, as such, has benefited to an amazing extent and we can only hope that her twin-sister, reason, will in due course assert herself.

CHAPTER IV

HEREDITY AND INSTINCT

They say there is divinity in odd numbers, either in nativity, chance or death.
THE MERRY WIVES OF WINDSOR, *Act* v, *i.*

THE fact that two and two make four has been so familiar an idea to all of us, from childhood onwards, that we have probably never realized its true mathematical value, nor the difficulty of its acceptance by prehistoric man. That two apples and two apples make four apples: that two sheep and two sheep make four sheep: and that two men and two men make four men were matters of individual experience, which any man, at any time, could settle experimentally for himself by recourse to his own fingers. that two sheep and two apples should make a total of four units was an altogether different proposition.

The basis of all arithmetic undoubtedly lies in the primitive habit of counting on one's fingers—the development to count up to five was gradual; then from five to ten; and thence ten to twenty. Twenty was called a score and represented a whole man, with his ten fingers and ten toes. The practice of counting by the score, still survives in a few country districts but the old rhyming score is now almost extinct. Instead of using the ordinary numerals, our forefathers employed the semi-mnemonic "Eena, deena, dina, dus; Catla, weela, weila, wuss" and so on, up to twenty. In this way it was much simpler to count up to three score and ten, than to count up to seventy.

The evolution of counting, then, has been spread over a long period of time and has, in fact, now become instinctive. When we are born, instead of starting where our parents left off, we have to accumulate facts for ourselves, but the ancestral memory has never been extinguished; in fact, each generation has added fresh fuel to the fire and we pass on to our children the hereditary experience, accumulated through life by ourselves and our ancestors. Thus, by a process of evolution, counting has become a natural instinct and the infant born today commences life with the "gift of figuring". That does not mean to say that he is born a mathematician but it does mean to say that he has inherited a certain aptitude to become a mathematician or calculator.

What part does heredity play in making a person what he is? Medical men tell us that we are more likely to inherit a tendency towards acquiring certain diseases than we are to inherit the actual disease. Similarly, we may not inherit the ability to perform in detail certain mental operations but we do, undoubtedly, inherit the general *tendency* to carry out such mental operations. Calculating ability is possibly an organic power, inherent in each one of us, which has been lost through misuse but is capable of redevelopment by conscious effort.

Many influential thinkers have maintained that memory comes to us in inherited form and the apparently spontaneous outbreaks of arithmetical genius, in the most unlikely places, are possibly due to this inherited aptitude. Mathematical knowledge, with its practical applications, has increased during the past few centuries with accelerated progress. Figure-consciousness is universally prevalent, and future generations may well see the evolution of many Einsteins, and the solution of many philosophical and scientific problems, all inextricably associated with the theory of numbers.

No one will question the facts of inherited tendencies with such information available as that concerning the Mozart and Bach families in music and the Huxleys and Darwins in science. Not always can the traces of heredity be so clearly discerned, however, and our knowledge of the families and relatives of calculating boys is very limited. We *do* know that such masters as Safford and Gauss came from parents gifted far beyond the average, with mathematical ability. The "younger Bidder" might well have rivalled his father as a calculator had he made mathematics his chief study.

The inheritance of physical tendencies is much easier to trace than that of mental tendencies. Take the sex-linked character known as hæmophilia. When blood is shed it should clot, for the clot plugs the severed blood vessel and prevents bleeding to death. Some people are born with the lack of the power of the blood to clot—several of the royal families of Europe were plagued with this trouble. Inability of the blood to clot shows itself in males, never in females, but it is always transmitted by females. There is in each one of us what Thomas Hardy described as "the eternal thing in man that heeds no call to die"—things eternal passed on to us by our forbears—and this applies equally to mental as to physical attributes. We must not assume, however, that heredity and instinct are infallible and capable of no modification. As William James points out, this is a complete delusion. He says: "Instinct, as a rule, is very rough and ready, able to achieve its results under ordinary circumstances, but easily misled by anything unusual. Chicks follow their mother by instinct, but when they are quite young they will follow, with equal readiness, any moving object remotely resembling their mother, or even a human being."

THE BERNOULLI FAMILY TREE

A most striking example of the part played by heredity in mathematics is that of the Bernoulli family, which in three generations produced eight mathematicians of more than average ability. It is said that no fewer than 120 of the descendants have been traced genealogically and of this considerable posterity the majority achieved distinction.

The records of the family date from 1583 when as refugees from Antwerp and Alva they settled at Frankfort, and afterwards at Basel, where all but Daniel were born. James (1654–1705) versifier in Latin, French and German, self-taught in geometry, published tables on dialling, a system of teaching mathematics to the blind, a treatise on comets (1680); visited England, where he knew Boyle; discussed the weight of the air (1683); and professed mathematics at the University of Basel (1687). From a hint of Leibnitz's he developed and made his own the differential calculus; solved the problem of the logarithmic spiral (1690), of the isochronous curve, catenary, and of isoperimetrical figures (1696), over which he quarrelled with his brother John; applied the calculus of probabilities to life and its accidents and prepared the way for Lagrange's calculus of variations. His collected works were published at Geneva in 1744.

John (1667–1748) brother of James was for ten years a professor of mathematics at Groningen and his brother's successor at Basel. He was a rival of Newton and Leibnitz and excelled in differential, integral, and especially exponential calculus. He sided with Descartes, as James, his brother, did with Newton. He wrote on navigation, the planets and the laws of motion. His works were published at Geneva in 1742 and his correspondence with Leibnitz in 1745.

Daniel (1700–1782) was born at Groningen, and was proud to call himself "the son of John Bernoulli". He published his first treatise in mathematics in 1724; was professor of mathematics at St. Petersburg (1725–1732); wrote his treatise *Hydrodynamica* in 1738, the first on the subject in which he advocated the Bernoulli system of propulsion for ships; was professor at different times of anatomy, physics, botany and filled the chair of natural and of speculative philosophy at Basel.

Not so distinguished as the above, but none the less men of mark were Nicholas (1687–1759), professor of mathematics at Padua; John (1710–1790) wrote on the capstan, magnetism and light; John (1744–1807), astronomer-royal of Berlin at nineteen; Jerome (1715–1829), a naturalist; James (1759–1789), professor of physics at Basel; Christopher (1782–1863), professor of natural history at Basel. The most significant feature concerning most of the mathematical members of this family in the second and third generations is that they did not deliberately choose mathematics as a profession but drifted into it in spite of themselves.

The part played by heredity, in regard to mathematical genius, would not be complete without further reference to Pascal, the inventor of the first calculating machine. He can, perhaps, hardly be described as a calculating boy but he would certainly come well within the category of calculating youths.

CHAPTER V

DEVELOPMENT

A witty statesman said, you might prove anything by figures.   THOMAS CARLYLE.

To what extent is the gift for calculating (in-so-far as it concerns calculating boys) due to experience or education? Binet gave eight years as the average age of a "natural" calculator, but Mitchell thought this too high. There is little doubt that the precocity of calculators has occasioned considerable uncritical speculations on these matters. We must observe that the age at which a calculator may have been exhibited to the public is not, necessarily, the age at which his gifts blazed forth. Indeed, it is doubtful whether there has been any "blazing forth" in the usual acceptance of the expression, at any time.

In the nature of things, every calculator must have gone through a more or less extended period of training or education. In the early stages of development, in particular, detailed explanations of the problems would be required. No boy could extract a cube root without being told just what he was to do and, perhaps, with some suggestions as to the best way to set about it. The time taken and the mental energy expended in learning "how to do it" would be reflected in the speed and accuracy with which he eventually did do it! It was this period of training, combined with unusual arithmetical and memorizing ability that resulted in the production of the prodigy.

It has been urged that to understand the precocity of calculators we must not lose sight of the fact that arithmetic is one of the most independent and self-sufficient of all the sciences. Given a knowledge of how to count and the necessary instructions of the operations to be mastered, any child of average ability can go on, once his interest is aroused, and construct unaided practically the whole science of arithmetic, no matter how much or how little he knows of other things.

In accordance with the usual tendency of all mental operations, shortenings of the processes involved will come with practice so that, in favourable cases, the whole process may eventually become, in a large measure, automatic. Indeed, the interest in counting may seem so natural to the child that he may assume that everyone else possesses this gift and it may be years before he realizes the actual facts. There may well be numerous "would have been" prodigies who, through accident or chance, have never been discovered.

In studying the training and development of calculators, it is very clear that mental calculation and mathematical ability are entirely independent of each other. On the other hand, lack of general knowledge does appear to have considerable effect on mental training. It is probable that the very fact that a child was stupid in other directions may have resulted in his concentration on the subject he liked and in which he was able to excel. As his all-round knowledge increased and his interests widened it was often the case that his ability in mental calculation weakened and, in some cases, was completely lost.

It has already been suggested that calculators could be made. If he devoted his whole time to arithmetical training, mentally, a boy of ordinary intelligence might eventually rival the exhibitions of the prodigies. The French mentalist, Dagbert, is an excellent example of the force of this argument.

EXPERIMENTS ON MEMORY

An interesting article appeared in the September, 1936, issue of the American magazine—*Popular Science Monthly*

(Bib. 20). It arose out of a visit to the Ohio State University of Dr. Salo Finkelstein. Dr. Finkelstein, a Polish mathematical specialist, was hired by an American broadcasting company to tally returns of the 1932 Presidential election because, it is stated, he was faster than an adding machine. His stay at Ohio State University lengthened to a year and a half, while research workers subjected him to various tests. One of their objects was to discover the secret of his prodigious memory for numbers.

When Dr. Finkelstein arrived at the University it took him 17½ seconds to memorize twenty-five numerals arranged in rows and columns of a square. He could repeat these vertically, horizontally or in any order called for. It is stated that the world's record for this feat, of a shade under 13 seconds, was held by a German mathematician. Before Finkelstein had completed his experiments with the psychologists, however, he had accomplished the feat of committing a twenty-five number square to memory in less than nine seconds. The value of experiments such as this, is vitiated by the absence of details. For example the account in *Popular Science Monthly* does not state whether the numerals were called out, separately and distinctly (this would take possibly twenty seconds) or whether they were already written on a blackboard. In any case, this looks suspiciously like the mnemonic chart favoured by magicians.

In continuation of the experiments with Finkelstein at the Ohio State University, we are told, that the psychologists in these experiments set themselves the problem of discovering whether an average person could become a memory expert. With college students as material they tried making number prodigies to order. It is said that "H.W.", one of their subjects, received seventy-five hours of special training, after which he proceeded to astonish even his instructors. It took Dr. Finkelstein 4·43 seconds to learn by heart the number 624,706,845,986,193,261,832

—less time than it takes to read the number aloud! "H.W.", we are told, managed the same feat in 4·37 seconds.

Popular Science Monthly does not recommend what it describes as "mental crutches" (*i.e.* mnemonics). It claims this is bad because it gives the mind the task of handling two types of material at one time. It is also claimed that a subject trained to study combinations of digits, instead of combinations of letters, can read long numbers, at a glance, just as long words can be read without, knowingly, stopping to read each individual letter. It is stated that this proved to be the secret of the number wizardry that Dr. Finkelstein displayed to the University experimenters. He had simply learned to view a long number as a string of smaller, three-digit figures, which were as easily recognizable to him as English words are to an average Englishman. It gave him, we are told, no more trouble to memorize a number like 312,655,135,354,697,255,817 than an ordinary individual would have in memorizing a string of simple three-letter words. It might, of course, be stated as argument in favour of this method that there are only ten different figures as against twenty-six different letters in the alphabet. In spite of the arguments brought forward above the author's inclination is strongly in favour of the mnemonic method of memorizing. "Mental crutches"; or mnemonics have enabled him to perform feats of memory which he would have found quite impossible without some such help.

LEARNING TO CALCULATE

We have ample proof. that general knowledge has no relation to arithmetical ability. This is evidenced by the large percentage of illiterate prodigies—and not only illiterate, but even feeble-minded. In this connection mention has already been made of P. Donym, in England and Verhaeghe in Belgium. Professor Elliott also tells of a half-idiot who was remarkable in his own district for his powers of calculation. He got him to put down his operations, in a few cases, on paper and states that his methods of abbreviation were very ingenious.

It is most probable that under cultivation the power of mental calculation could be greatly developed. The immense saving of time, in school and afterwards, that would result from an ability to shorten the associations, to use a multiplication table of two figures, and above all to register mentally, should be sufficient to justify a trial.

Fuller, Ampère, Bidder, Mondeux, Buxton, Gauss, Whately, Colburn and Safford, learned numbers and their values before figures, just as a child learns words and their meanings long before he can read. Bidder declared emphatically: "The reason for my obtaining the peculiar power of dealing with numbers may be attributed to the fact that I knew the value of numbers before I knew the symbolical figures. . . . In consequence of this, numbers have always had a significance and meaning to me, very different from that which the figures convey to children in general."

Ampère, Bidder and Mondeux learned their arithmetic from pebbles. Arago says of Ampère: "It may be that he had fallen upon the ingenious method of the Hindoos, or perhaps his pebbles were combined like the corn strung upon parallel lines by the Brahmin mathematicians of Pondicherry, Calcutta and Benares and handled by them with such rapidity, precision and accuracy."

If we would do away with the mystery of calculation, perhaps the value of numbers and the tables might then become so indelibly fixed in the minds of children and so easy of multiplication that they could also do long "sums" mentally, or even carry the two-figure multiplication tables in their heads.

Short-cuts, both psychological and arithmetical must partly, if not wholly, account for the speed attained by some of the prodigies in their mental calculations. Problems done instantly are either very simple, or else they are solved by guess and trial with the aid of little tricks and properties discovered by the calculators. Another aspect to bear in mind is that a prodigy giving exhibitions, perhaps daily, must of necessity have many repetitions and the solutions, or routines, or both may have been memorized.

Owing to the origin of mental calculation in ordinary counting and the complete independence and self-sufficiency of mental arithmetic, mere arithmetical precocity falls in a different class from musical precocity, and still more from the all-round precocity of such men as Ampère and Macaulay. If, for any reason, the arithmetical prodigy loses his interest in calculation, or the opportunity to practise it, his power is likely to diminish or eventually to disappear. In this respect, mental calculation is like piano-playing, or any other highly specialized activity dependent on long practice.

Gauss remarks that in the ability to reckon rapidly two things must be distinguished—a powerful memory and a real ability for calculation. He was of the opinion that these two qualities were entirely independent of each other. They can be united, but are not always so. Bidder's opinion was that mental calculation depends on two faculties of the mind in simultaneous operation—computing and registering the result.

Euler had a prodigious memory for everything. This gave him the power of performing long mathematical operations in his head. While instructing his children, the extraction of roots obliged him to give them numbers which were squares; these he reckoned out in his head. Troubled by insomnia, one night he calculated the first six powers of all the numbers under 20, and recited them several days afterwards.

There is a fascination in "fiddling" with figures which

increases and develops with practice. Bidder looked upon figures as his friends. Prodigies are not the only ones to derive untold pleasure from excursions into this realm. This pleasure comes within the same category as that derived from chess and the solution of crossword puzzles. There is probably some psychological explanation for this tendency which, at the moment, remains obscure.

CHAPTER VI

VISILES, AUDILES AND MOTILES

*Nay, Madam, when you are declaiming, declaim: and
when you are calculating, calculate.*

SAMUEL JOHNSON.

MOST people think, or imagine, by means of mental pictures.
When we speak of someone possessing a vivid imagination,
we mean an individual who is able to picture an object
or scene, in the mind's eye, as vividly as if he saw it before
him. These pictorial images are often most elusive and it
is not surprising that many people do not appear to have
the least idea of the process of thinking.

Subjects of the visual type were classified by Francis
Galton as visiles and those of the auditory type, he named
audiles. The person whose preferred type of imagery is
motor or kineasthetic is known as a motile. *Mind* (xi.415)
gives another category described as "indifferents" but it
will be found that the three types of imagery, or a combination of two or all of these, will cover the ground. It
has been said that the person who is neither audile, visile
nor motile must be a microcephalous idiot!

Try it now for yourself by doing a simple sum in mental
arithmetic. If you are multiplying 8 by 4 you will find,
if you are a visile and if you give it sufficiently close attention,
that you visualize in your mind these two figures. If you
concentrate and do not allow extraneous thoughts to
intrude; that is, if you attend to what you are doing you
will do it much better than if you allow the mind to wander.
Likewise, if you want to recollect, say, a song or a tune,
your mind goes through the same process but in this case
you mentally hear. No hard and fast line can be drawn
between visiles and audiles. In bringing to mind, say, a

public speaker most of us, mentally both see his face and hear his voice.

Among the leading calculators, visiles and audiles are almost equally divided. Inaudi was in no doubt whatever that he heard the replies to the questions put to him. On the other hand, Bidder states: "If I perform a sum mentally, it always proceeds in a visible form in my mind: indeed, I cannot conceive of any other way possible of doing mental arithmetic."

Among calculators generally, and those with no special arithmetical ability, visiles are met with more frequently than audiles. Most people by reading a letter for themselves can pick up the points much quicker than by hearing it read to them by someone else. Among prodigies in particular one occasionally meets with that curious phenomenon known as a photographic memory. A mere glance leaves a mental image from which detail may later be gathered at will.

Bidder had a very vivid imagination. He had the faculty of carrying about with him a mental picture of the numbers, figures, diagrams etc., with which he was occupied and he saw, as if it were on a slate, the problem he was working on. He had the capacity for seeing, as if photographed on his retina, the exact figures with which he was occupied.

Colburn said that when making his calculations, he saw them clearly before him. It is said of Buxton that he preserved the several processes of multiplying the multiplicand by each figure of the lower line in their relative order and place, as on paper, until the final product was found.

MEMORY AND CALCULATION

The importance of distinguishing between memory and calculation has frequently been stressed. It has become customary in the literature on mathematical prodigies to distinguish, more or less sharply, the parts played by memory and by calculation proper in the various operations, especially where the numbers dealt with are very long. Bidder tells us that only the limits of his memory would stand in the way of performing immense calculations, in an incredible short time. Buxton was excessively slow in calculating but had such a tenacious memory that he could work on a problem for weeks and so solve any problem, long or short, that happened to arouse his interest.

"Now it can hardly be questioned that the mathematical prodigy's figure-memory is superior to the ordinary man's," says Mitchell. "Dealing constantly with figures, the mental calculator learns to assimilate them readily. A twenty-figure number, which for most of us is a meaningless string of figures, devoid of interest, for him 'makes sense', and so is easy to learn. Hence, we may safely assume that the calculator's figure-memory will outstrip his powers of calculations. By the time he can mentally multiply two six-figure numbers, he will have little or no trouble in remembering, almost at a glance, or after a single hearing, two numbers of seven or eight figures each."

Myers points out that the ignorant prodigies seldom appear to have been conscious of any continuous logical process, while in some cases the separation of the supra-liminal and subliminal trains of thought must have been very complete. He quotes that Buxton would talk freely whilst doing his questions, that being no molestation or hindrance to him. Fixity and clearness of inward visualization seems to have been the leading necessity in all these achievements. It apparently mattered little whether the mental blackboard on which the steps of the calculation were recorded was or was not visible to the mind's eye of the supraliminal self.

Intense concentration does not seem to be so necessary

to the calculating boy, nor does the evidence available
suggest that these boys were "dreamers". It would appear
that the ability to see vivid visual images is in no way
dependent on the ability to concentrate. It is well known that
a person of feeble mind is poor at concentration, and quite
a large percentage of calculators fall within this category.

A child may begin to learn his three-times table by
imaginary numbers, on a mental slate, until eventually
the process becomes so automatic that he loses all knowledge
of the preliminary steps. This is illustrated by the statements
of many of the calculators that they do not know "how
they do it". It is likely, indeed it is most probable, that
there are many boys who do not know "they could do it"
who, under favourable circumstances might develop into
prodigies. They might well go through life without sus-
pecting that they possessed arithmetical gifts of an unusual
nature. If the psychologists are right, in some instances,
the gift might emerge in some other form. On the other
hand, the gift of mental calculation may well be the sub-
lineation of some other ability.

DURATION OF CALCULATING FACULTY

This brings us to another aspect and that is the comparatively short duration of the ability to see with the
mind's eye, or hear with the mind's ear to the unusual
extent possessed by calculators. Among calculators of low
or average intelligence, the gift has usually lasted for a
few years only—an average of five years would probably
be on the high side. On the other hand, in a few exceptional
cases, such as Bidder and Inaudi, the gift lasted a lifetime.

Mr. Van R. of Utica, at the age of six years distinguished
himself in mental calculation. At eight, he entirely lost this
faculty, and after that time he could calculate neither
better nor faster than any other person. He did not retain

the slightest idea of the manner in which he performed his calculations in childhood.

Referring to two men of high ability who possessed the gift of mental calculation, Professor Safford and Archbishop Whately, Myers was struck by the evanescence of the power after early youth—or even before the end of childhood. Whately, in referring to his powers said: "There was certainly something peculiar in my calculating faculty. It began to show itself between five and six, and lasted about three years. . . . I soon got to do the most difficult sums, always in my head, for I knew nothing of figures beyond numeration. I did these sums much quicker than anyone could do on paper, and I never remember committing the smallest error. When I went to school, at which time the passion wore off, I was a perfect dunce in ciphering, and have continued so ever since."

"Still more remarkable, perhaps," says Myers, "was Professor Safford's loss of power. Professor Safford's whole bent was mathematical; his boyish gift of calculation raised him into notice and he became a Professor of Astronomy. He had, therefore, every motive and every opportunity to retain the gift, if thought and practice could have retained it. But, whereas at ten years old he worked correctly in his head, in one minute, a multiplication sum whose answer consisted of 36 figures he was, later in life, neither more nor less capable of such calculation than his neighbours."

By way of explaining the loss of power, Mitchell observes that mental calculation starts from an interest in counting. At the outset, it demands only that ability to count by 1's, 2's, 3's, 7's and the like which all of us require for everyday purposes such as keeping track of time and the days of the week, etc. If, for any reason, the interest in counting is lost, the skill already acquired will disappear.

CHAPTER VII

THE TIME FACTOR

See Mystery to Mathematics fly!
ALEXANDER POPE.

THE two most prominent aspects of the powers possessed
by calculators is the ability to memorize figures and the
ability to perform the operations of mental arithmetic with
extreme rapidity. A study of the times taken to carry out
the various calculations will prove that in the majority of
instances the operations were performed, mentally, with
much greater rapidity than an ordinary person could do
similar operations on paper, in the usual way. To some
extent, speed may be due to constant practice but that
covers only a portion of the ground. Concentration, in the
case of these mental calculations appears to have very little
to do with the result. It almost looks as though we shall
have to seek the explanation from a consideration of that
region so popular with most psychologists—the subconscious
mind.

THE SUBCONSCIOUS MIND

Many years ago, the author carried out a series of
experiments on subjects under hypnosis. There was one
subject in particular, who, "under the influence", excelled in
mental calculation. Had it been possible to devote sufficient
time to his training it is believed that he would eventually
have become a competitor of the calculating boys. One
got the impression that the speed with which these calculations were performed was due to the subconscious mind

being able to operate without interference from the conscious mind. It seemed that whilst under hypnosis the subject had a single-track mind. When doing these sums, he was a calculator and a calculator only, mentally free from all other matters that might distract his attention.

It is, of course, well known from hypnotic experiments that the subconscious mind has the remarkable faculty of counting and estimating time. Dr. J. Milne Bramwell placed on record some interesting experiments. It was suggested to one of his subjects, whilst in the hypnotic sleep, that at the expiration of 11,470 minutes, whatever might happen, she would make a cross on paper and note the time. Out of 55 similar experiments, 45 were completely successful.

How true it may be we cannot say but it is a popular assertion that when a man is drowning his past life comes before him instantaneously. It may happen that many memories course through the brain in a second of time. Sir William Hamilton, in his *Lectures on Metaphysics* (*p.* 236), designates the phenomenon as "latent memory". He says: "The evidence on this point shows that the mind frequently contains whole systems of knowledge, which, though in our normal state they have faded into oblivion, may, in certain abnormal states . . . flash out into luminous consciousness, and even throw into the shade of unconsciousness those other systems by which they had, for a long period, been eclipsed and even extinguished. For example, there are cases in which the extinct memory of whole languages was suddenly restored; and, what is even still more remarkable, in which the faculty was exhibited of accurately repeating, in known or unknown tongues, passages which were never in the grasp of conscious memory in the normal state."

Coleridge, in his *Biographia Literaria*, tells of a servant girl, resident in a small town in Germany, who, in a state of fever, "continued incessantly talking Latin, Greek and Hebrew in very pompous tones and with most distinct enunciation". At the time, she was 24 years of age and could neither read nor write. It appeared that at the age of nine she was taken into the house of an old Protestant pastor, and had remained there until the old man's death. It had been the custom of the old gentleman, for years, to walk up and down a passage in his house, into which the kitchen door opened, and to read to himself, with a loud voice, out of his favourite books. The old pastor was a very learned man and the physician attending the servant girl was eventually able to trace in his collection several books in which he identified many passages with those taken down at the young woman's bedside.

Bidder's account of the rapidity of his mental calculations has been quoted earlier (*pp.* 82, 83).

Time and space, under the action of certain drugs, seem non-existent. The theory of relativity tends to show that, in the usually accepted sense of the word, time is a delusion; it regards time as a fourth dimension.

The most striking proof of a time-sense, is that provided by the experiments on subjects under hypnosis. From personal experience, the author is convinced that many of the remarkable claims in this connection have not been exaggerated. Professor Bernheim (*Suggestive Therapeutics*) says of one of his subjects: "I made A say that he would come back to me in thirteen days at ten o'clock in the morning. He remembered nothing when he waked. On the thirteenth day, at ten o'clock in the morning, he appeared, having come three kilometres from his house to the hospital. He had been working in a foundry all night: went to bed at six in the morning and woke up at nine with the idea that he had to come to the hospital to

see me. He told me that he had no such idea on the preceding days, and did not know he had to come to see me.
It came into his head just at the time when he ought to
carry it out."

The relation of the subconscious, say, to bodily processes
is very involved but that does not prevent us from
carrying out these processes instantaneously. For example,
the act of putting pencil to paper involves the transmission
to and from the brain of complicated messages through the
nerves. The number of cells concerned in the action runs
into many thousands but the process is performed in an
instant of time.

As regards the psychological aspect of time, in the
Sunday Express for 17 October, 1943, F. W. Nitardy put
forward an interesting theory on the apparent speeding-up
of time with advancing age. He wrote:

"The apparent acceleration of time as one grows
older seems a universal experience. All of us can recall
what a long time a year used to seem when we were
young children and how, as we grow older, the years
seem to pass faster. A year in our twenties seemed a
much longer space of time than a year in our forties,
and as we approach sixty the year seems to be shorter
still.

The reason . . . of this apparent acceleration of time
with age . . . might lie in that elapsed time, as measured
by the recollection of an individual, seemed long or
short according to what relationship it had to his total
time experience. For instance, at the age of eight, when
our memory might go back over four years, a year would
represent 25 per cent of our total remembered time
experience, and hence might seem like a very long time.
At the age of 12, the memory might go back over eight
years, and one year would represent 12½ per cent of the

total remembered time experience and could, therefore, appear only half as long as a year did at the age of eight.

Similarly, at the age of 15, a year would be likely to represent only about ten per cent of remembered time and seem still shorter. At the age of 25 it would represent only about 5 per cent of remembered time, and hence seem only half as long as at the age of 15. At the age of 45, a year would represent only 2½ per cent of remembered time, and at the age of 60, only 2 per cent, or less. Thus, as the years roll by, time would seem to be accelerating in speed."

The following little paradox may serve to illustrate the difficulty in reaching a perfectly clear understanding of the relation between time and space. One Sunday morning a man set out to walk from his home to church two miles away. He made the journey in stages, each stage being half the distance and occupying half the time of the one immediately preceding. Thus, the first stage of one mile occupied twenty minutes, the second stage of half a mile took ten minutes, the third stage of a quarter of a mile took five minutes and so on. How long would it take him to complete the journey? On a time basis, it might be argued that the complete journey would take forty minutes, but as each stage is only half the distance of the one immediately preceding, in theory, the journey would never be completed. The fallacy of such arguments will be obvious to anyone who understands the theory of geometrical progression. The time required to complete the journey consists of an infinite number of terms, but these get smaller and smaller, and the sum of them all is a finite time. After the lapse of that time the journey would be completed. (*See also p.* 217.)

Many years ago, the author lapsed into verse on this

question of time and space. He cannot refrain from inflicting it upon the reader. Here it is:

TIME-SPACE

If everything involving time
    Were speeded up a hundred fold,
In four months, man would reach his prime:
    In eight, he would be growing old.

A year would still seem just the same,
    Although it would not last four days;
Eternity, is but a name—
    It does not help us through the maze.

Thus, when we come to think of size,
    A mote might well a world contain:
This earth of ours, we realize,
    Is, relatively, but a grain.

Length, and the like, one reconciles
    With former notions of a pace:
An inch may be a million miles,
    In the infinity of space.

Countless as sand specks on the shore,
    Worlds have evolved; we know not how,
Never shall be when time's no more,
    'Tis all an everlasting now.

Suppose that something did take place—
    Say, if the gods employed their wit
To play about with this time-space,
    We'd probably not know of it!

SECTION II

ASSOCIATED PHENOMENA

CHAPTER VIII

CHESS PRODIGIES

We are but chess-men in a game of chess
Played by great heaven in its waywardness,
Hither and thither on the board we move,
And singly reach the box of nothingness.

OMAR KHAYYAM.

THERE is a close resemblance between calculators and
chess prodigies. In each case, we have a wide variation of
powers from the highly skilled man of general all-round
ability to the comparatively illiterate person with a one-
track mind. It is proposed to make only a passing reference
to the wonders performed by the masters and prodigies
of chess, and to devote our space to a study of the likeness
between chess and calculation.

It will be taken for granted that the reader has some
knowledge of the game, but even if his acquaintance with
the various moves and objects is entirely elementary, it
should not seriously interfere with his ability to follow the
points that will be considered.

For the information of the uninstructed, chess may be
likened to a sham-fight on a battle-ground of 64 squares.
Sixteen men are employed on each side, varying in rank
from the king to foot soldier, and each type of fighter has
his own particular moves. The purpose of each player is
to checkmate his opponent; that is, to hem in the king in
such a manner that he cannot escape being captured.

The game of chess is almost as old and as universal as
the game of figuring—pawns were discovered in the tomb

of Tutankhamen, sealed 1400 B.C. Both are intellectual recreations in the true sense of the term, with the curious anomaly that skill in calculation and skill in chess is in neither case any proof, or even indication, of general intelligence. In both cases, we have many examples of persons of otherwise low mentality, and even of feeble mind, being skilful at calculation, or chess, as the case may be.

Psychologists tell us that the world-wide popularity of chess is due to its appeal to the fundamental instinct of combat. It is a grand battle, without any of the unfortunate features of the real thing. It is an exercise of intellectual skill as opposed to physical dexterity. It appeals to the fighting instincts of the player and invites him to match his skill against that of his opponent. As a player of no more than average ability, the author has derived many hours of pleasure from chess and, rightly or wrongly, is convinced that his acquaintance with the game has stood him in good stead in the more serious business of life.

Without going into details, let us say that the game of chess calls, in particular, for foresight and visualization—foresight in being able to plan moves ahead and visualization in building up a mental image of the position ahead. In particular, visualization is called into play in working out chess problems, mentally, without the board or men, such problems, for example, as are to be found in newspapers and magazines, where white is told to "play and mate in three moves", etc.

It would appear that certain mental qualities are essential to the player who would attain any degree of proficiency. Master players,. combine to a marked degree an accurate chess-memory, quickness of perception, a constructive imagination, concentration, power of accurate analysis and ability to foresee what will be the probable position several moves ahead.

Many volumes could be written of the wonderful achievements of experienced chess players, who are rightly called "masters". The expert displays his skill in simultaneous games; that is, playing several games at one time against as many opponents, blindfold play, in which the player is dependent entirely on his ability to memorize and visualize; blindfold simultaneous play; and in repeating from memory all the moves that have been made.

To give an example of simultaneous play; the author saw a Polish boy, of about eleven years of age, play twenty simultaneous games with skilled players. Apart from chess, this boy had no particular ability. He moved quickly and won 17 games, losing 1 and leaving 2 unfinished. One curious thing in this match was that the boy seemed to pay more attention to the features of his opponent than to the board. He gazed earnestly into the face of each opposing player and the game he lost was where his opponent studiously avoided looking him in the face! This child would come in the category of chess prodigies. There have been many such and, as already mentioned, they resemble in many ways the mathematical prodigies previously discussed.

The ability of a player to dictate from memory all the moves made by himself and his opponent is, of course, a feat of memory, pure and simple. It is recorded of the chess master, Paul Morphy, that the morning after a contest against eight other players, in Paris, he was able to dictate to his secretary all the moves in each of the eight games. Morphy stated that of the many thousands of games he had played, after his chess powers were mature, he had not forgotten a single game.

The performance of what is known as "the knight's tour" is often claimed to be something remarkable. This consists of placing the knight on any designated square and, without seeing the board, calling out each successive move until every square on the board has been covered. This achievement is on a par with that of many magical "lightning" calculations in that a player of average ability, by memorizing certain simple rules, can readily duplicate it.

It is the blindfold players who, justly, get most of the applause. Alfred A. Cleveland (Bib. 1), states that Paul Morphy, during his triumphant tour of Europe, created great astonishment by playing eight simultaneous games blindfold. It is said, by competent judges, that some of his most brilliant games were played in this way. Cleveland states that the American player, Pillsbury, played as many as twenty-two blindfold games simultaneously, winning most of them.

CHESS AND GENERAL ABILITY

We cannot do better than quote A. A. Cleveland on the relation of chess skill to general mental ability. He says:

"If chess is perhaps a tolerable index of temperament and character, is skill in chess also a reliable index of mental power in general? The reply must be qualified. Many able men are good chess players, but on the other hand there are those who live for chess; who think, talk and dream chess; who confirm Edgar Allen Poe's observation that the best chess player may be only the best player at chess; but this number is small compared to the vast majority who indulge in it only as a pastime.

"Even among chess masters are to be found many who have displayed considerable ability in other directions. Dr. Emanuel Lasker, the one-time world's champion at chess took his doctorate in mathematics, Tschigorin was a Russian government employee, Maroczy was Professor of physics and mathematics at a Budapest college, Tarrasch was a German physician, Anderson, at one time champion of the world, was a professor of mathematics, and Staunton, another world's champion and one of the best known of the older chess writers, was well known also as a writer and as an editor of the classics.

"Rousseau, Voltaire, Napoleon, and John Stuart Mill are said to have been strong players, and the historian Buckle an excellent one. This list might be increased indefinitely, but enough has been said to indicate that skilful chess players represent all walks of life, and that skill at chess is not incompatible with success in other lines. The chess player is usually something more than a mere player of chess.

"At the same time, the cases of *idiots savants* in various forms of mental activity and, amongst others, in chess playing, prevent the inference that skill in chess is a universally valid index of high mental endowment."

In an appendix to his work, Cleveland gives details of a chess player of fair ability who was feeble-minded and an inmate of an American asylum.

Cleveland also draws an analogy between the chess expert and the mathematician "who has merely to glance at a formula, or at its first two or three terms, in order to recognize its full import. Every situation in a game of chess which requires readjustment of the player's plans is a problem for him, and the quickness and accuracy of his solution will depend upon his ability to seize upon the salient and essential features and to neglect those which have no meaning for that particular situation.

"Obviously, the mathematician's skill, when confronted by a problem, will display itself in his ability to recognize the fundamental nature of the problem. Lindley found that an expert mathematician among those who attempted to solve his puzzle, recognized at a glance the mathematical principle involved and solved it without difficulty. He displayed what corresponds to 'position sense' in chess. The chess player has this advantage. In any particular game he has built up or helped to build up his own problem and has a mental record of its progress. He has seen the possibility of certain lines of play eliminated one by one and is thus able to concentrate on the remaining ones."

Psychologists, in general, appear to agree that chess playing may become, in course of time, purely automatic. The player, by means of many repetitions learns a series of moves in regular sequence and, according to his skill, eventually makes use of short-cuts. In this again, we see the resemblance to mental calculations; in fact, chess *is* a form of mental calculation. It has its child prodigies, just as arithmetic and music. Capablanca, chess champion of the world from 1921–27, started to play chess at the age of four.

We close this chapter with a delightful little incident taken from *Mathematical Recreations* (Bib. 17). Maurice Kraitchik, the author, to demonstrate his contention that mathematics is applied logic in its simplest and purest form, says:

"I have long been an ardent chess player, yet my twelve-year old daughter scarcely knows the moves. (The reader may be assured, he need not know them either.) Recently two of my friends, who are chess experts, came to dinner. After dinner I played one game with each of them and lost both games, although against each I had the advantage of a pawn and the opening move. Just as we finished my daughter came into the room. On learning of my ill-success she said: 'Daddy, I'm ashamed of you. I can do better than that. Let me play them! I don't want any advantage— I'll play one game with white pieces and one with black. (In chess, the white pieces always move first.) And I'll give them an advantage by playing both games at once. Still, I shall make out better than you did.'

"We took her up immediately on this. To my mingled

delight and chagrin, she made good; she did better than I had. How did she do it?

"*Solution:* Let us call the experts Mr. White and Mr. Black, according to the colour of the pieces each played against my daughter. Mr. White played first. My daughter copied his first move as her opening against Mr. Black at the other board. When Mr. Black had answered this move, she copied his move at the first board as her reply to Mr. White. And so on. In this way, the simultaneous games against the two experts became a single game between them; my daughter served as a messenger to transmit the moves. Hence, she was certain that she would either win one game and lose the other, or draw both."

CHAPTER IX

MUSICAL PRODIGIES

"Eccentricities of genius, Sam," said Mr. Pickwick.

CHARLES DICKENS.

THE question has often been asked as to what happens
to the chess and musical child prodigies who, for a few
weeks, or months, are the centre of attention from press
and public and then, apparently, vanish into forgetfulness.
In calling attention to what he describes as a "trick of fate",
the author of an article in the *Birmingham Mail*, 8 February,
1946, stated:

"Over the past ten or twelve years scores of precocious
youngsters have been hailed as geniuses. Of these, how
many have made good their early promise? How many
are famous today?

Where is Andrew Nastell, of Faversham, a skilled
performer on the penny whistle at two and acclaimed an
accomplished musician at six? Does Folkestone's child
marvel, June Masters, a competent conductor at five,
now control her own orchestra? What fame today has
Arthur Greenwood of Brooklyn, U.S.A., who knew the
alphabet at one year old and at seven was more proficient than his masters at astronomy, chemistry and
physics?

Perhaps, strangest of all, was the infant known as
the 'Cradle Prophet', child of a peasant of Petallan,
Mexico, who talked immediately after birth in perfect
Spanish and predicted six months of calamities and
disasters. Probably he died; certainly he was never
heard of again.

Then there was the English child, Daisy Ashford,

whose book *The Young Visiters* (she spelt it 'Visiters') written at the age of nine and published some years later, was greeted as a masterpiece of its kind. No other great work has since been published by the same author.

These child wonders, and hundreds like them, had their brief day and then disappeared from public view. The young prodigies who throughout history fulfilled early expectations can be counted on the fingers of your hands.

Science looks on these child prodigies as 'sports'. They say that out of every 1000 children born, 50 are bright, 20 are brilliant and one only is a prodigy.

What is the key to this mystery? Medical experts explain it as a difference in constitution that is to be found in the glands, pituitary, pineal and adrenal. With these 'wonder children' certain portions of their nervous system reach peak activity long before the rest of the body. They live far too fast, and physique and emotions cannot keep pace with their brains.

In many cases these unfortunate children are literally worked to death. Too eager parents, or guardians, force them to concentrate on whatever particular subject they excel in, with the result that the child forgets the normal activities of youth and fails completely to adjust him or herself to the world around.

Child prodigies, it may be noted, are far more common in boys than in girls, and this may be due to the fact that infantile gland disorders are mainly to be found in males.

The special faculties that develop early most commonly seem to be those for music, mathematics and chess. These subjects do not require experience of life and creative ability. Much rarer are prodigies of painting or literature. The number of worth-while pictures painted or books written by children under 16 could be counted on the fingers of one hand."

The figure quoted for the estimated percentage of prodigies to the general population is far too high. Instead of one in a thousand, as suggested, one in a million would be more accurate. Nor is it altogether correct to say that most of the prodigies fade into oblivion. At least, not so far as child musical prodigies are concerned.

PRECOCIOUS MUSICIANS

Most musical prodigies were precocious in that they began their musical careers at a very tender age. Many of them descended from eminent musical families, as witness the Purcells, Bachs, Scarlattis, Mendelssohns and Wesleys. Let us consider some of the most famous musicians of all time:

Sebastian Bach (1685–1750) was a transcendent musical genius. He was very precocious and arrived at the full maturity of his powers at 22. His home life was simple and quiet. He was a good husband, father, friend and citizen. He was very laborious and became blind from over-study. The Bachs were a musical family comprising a vast number of individuals and extending through eight generations. It began in 1550; it culminated in Sebastian and its last known member was Regina Susanna, who was alive in 1800, but in indigent circumstances. There were many eminent musicians among the Bachs—the biographical collections of musicians gives the lives of no less than 57 of them (*See* Fetis *Dictionary of Musicians*). It was the custom of the family to meet in yearly reunions, at which the entertainments were purely musical. In or about 1750 as many as 120 Bachs attended one of these meetings.

Another musical prodigy was Charles Wesley who at the age of three surprised his father—also Charles, author of some six thousand hymns and brother of John the founder of Methodism—by playing a tune on the harpsichord, readily and in proper time. Whatever his mother sang, or whatever he heard in the streets he could without difficulty make out on this instrument. When he played by himself, his mother used to tie him by his back-string to the chair, in order to prevent his falling. Even at this age he always put a true bass to every tune he played and from the beginning he played without study or hesitation. When the boy was four years old, his father took him to London, where he was introduced to the foremost musicians of the time. When he was about six years old he was put under the tuition of a master in Bristol and, for some years, his study was almost entirely confined to the works of Corelli, Scarlatti and Handel. So rapid was his progress that it was thought that, at the age of twelve, no person was able to excel him in performing the compositions of these masters.

Samuel Wesley, brother of the preceding, was born in 1766 and he also gave a very early indication of musical genius. When only three years of age, he could play upon the organ; and, when eight years old attempted to compose an oratorio. The intellectual endowments of the adult Samuel Wesley were equal to his musical talents and his amiability and benevolence added lustre to his acquirements. He was described "a man of genius without pretension, and a good man without guile"—a beautiful and well-deserved epitaph. The Wesleys enriched the English language and music by the many hymns and tunes composed by this gifted family.

Richard Strauss wrote a polka and song at six and through a long life continued his musical compositions. In April 1950, television viewers in London and the Midlands had the privilege of seeing a film in which he was seen conducting an orchestra, playing one of his latest compositions. He was back again in his native country and it was stated that he was engaged on other compositions.

Yehudi Menuhin played the violin when he was three

years old and in 1948 at the age of 32 he was regarded as an outstanding violin virtuoso.

James Meyerbeer was exceedingly precocious. He played brilliantly at six and was among the best pianists of Berlin at nine. He began to publish compositions at 19 and died when he was 70.

In 1948, Pierino Gamba, at the age of ten, successfully conducted the Liverpool Philharmonic Orchestra and attracted large crowds at the Harringay Musical Festival. Hummel gave concerts at nine; Sir Landon Ronald could play the piano before he could speak. He lived to be 65.

At an International Psychical Congress in 1900, Professor Richet introduced Pepito Ariola, a three-and-a-half-years-old Spanish child, who could play classical pieces. He began playing the piano a year before and with his tiny hands he somehow managed to sound full octaves. It was claimed that "his hands appeared to grow while he played".

In the *Encyclopædia of Psychic Science* (Bib. 29) appears an account of Blind Tom, a negro child of South Georgia, almost an idiot, who played with both hands on the piano, using the black and white keys when only four years of age. He composed an original piece at five years old. He could play two tunes on the piano at the same time, one with each hand, while he sang a song in a different air. Each tune was set to a different key as dictated by the audience.

Any account of musical prodigies would be incomplete without the inclusion of some reference to the gifts of Wolfgang Amadeus Mozart (1756–1791). Mozart received practically all his education from his father, Leopold Mozart, musical director to the Archbishop of Salzburg. His sister, Maria Anna, who was five years older, was also a gifted pianist. At the time when his sister was beginning clavier practice, Wolfgang then three years old "was a constant attendant on her lessons and already showed by a fondness for striking thirds, a lively interest in music". At four years of age, he could always retain in his memory the brilliant solos in the concertos which he heard.

In 1762, when Wolfgang was six years old, after a gratifying reception at Munich and at the court of Vienna the trio, consisting of Mozart, his father and his sister, set out on a European tour which lasted several years, Wolfgang playing the piano, violin and organ, and everywhere creating a profound sensation.

In Paris, four of his sonatas for piano and violin were engraved, and before leaving London his father presented all Wolfgang's printed compositions to the British Museum, along with a motet which is his only work set to English words. For a considerable period subsequently, Mozart was taken on frequent tours throughout the Continent.

Mozart's reputation as a composer grew with his years; but his father's efforts to secure for him an appointment commensurate with his attainments were all in vain. In 1781 Mozart left home finally and settled in Vienna; but his marriage in 1782 to Constance Weber, a pianist and singer, increased the financial difficulties of his position and also brought upon him the wrath of his father.

Though always in the grinding grip of poverty, Mozart was constantly composing, and even to within a few hours of his death, was working at his unfinished Requiem. It is said that when asked by a friend as to the method by which he composed his sonatas and symphonies, Mozart replied:

"I do not myself know and can never find out. When I am in particularly good condition, perhaps riding in a carriage, or in a walk after a good meal, and in a sleepless night, then the thoughts come to me in a rush and best of all. Whence or how—that I do not know and cannot learn. Those which please me, I retain in my head and hum them perhaps to myself—at least, so others have told me. Then it goes on growing and I keep on expanding it and making it more distinct and the thing, however long it be, becomes almost finished in my head so that I afterwards survey it at a glance, like a goodly picture or handsome man, and in my imagination do not hear it at all in succession, as it afterwards must be heard, but as a simultaneous whole. That is indeed a feast! All the finding and making only goes on in me as in a very vivid dream." Mozart died at the age of 35 and left over six hundred works.

The list could be considerably extended. Given below in alphabetical order are some of the more prominent prodigies who gave evidence of their musical ability at a very tender age.

Berlioz (1803–1869) began to play and compose at the age of 14; Brahms (1833–1897) learnt the rudiments of music at a very early age; Chopin (1810–1849) when an infant, would weep at the sound of music and when 8 years of age played in public; Debussy (1862–1918) was a player and composer at the age of 11; Dvorak (1841–1904) played and composed at the age of 12; Handel (1685–1759) played on the clavicord when but an infant and was famous at the age of 5; Haydn (1732–1806) played and composed at the age of 6; Liszt (1811–1886) the son of a famous musician, played in public when only 9 years of age; Mendelssohn (1809–1847) also composed and played in public at the age of 9; Rossini (1792–1868) gave signs of musical genius at a very early age and performed in public at 14; Schubert (1797–1828) played in public at the age of 12; Verdi (1813–1901) was precocious as a youngster and performed in public at the age of 10; Wagner (1813–1833) conducted one of his own compositions in public when only 17 years of age; Weber (1786–1826) was taught to play and sing almost before he could talk and was appointed conductor of the Opera at Breslau when he was 17.

EFFORTLESS MASTERY

Professor Whiteley (Bib. 36) claims that the memory of a piece of music is in the hands and brain, not the mind, and when it is thoroughly learned there is an automatic correlation between seeing and playing; between one passage and the next.

This is a hard saying! Dr. Louis Berg (Bib. 30) is even more definite: "Involuntary actions—actions that have become automatic through experience and repetition—eventually become spinal in character and are caused by a simple spinal reflex arc, not involving the brain."

Samuel Butler, in referring to the art of playing the piano, in his *Life and Habit* says: "We observe that a practised player will perform very difficult pieces, apparently without effort; often indeed, while thinking and talking of something quite other than his music; yet he will play accurately and, possibly, with much expression. If he has been playing a fugue, say in four parts, he will have kept each part well distinct, in such a manner as to prove that his mind was not prevented, by its other occupations, from consciously or unconsciously following four distinct trains of musical thought at the same time, nor from making his fingers act in exactly the required manner as regards each note of each part.

"It commonly happens that in the course of four or five minutes a player will have struck four or five thousand notes. If we take into consideration the rests, dotted notes, accidentals, variations of time etc., we shall find his attention must have been exercised on many more occasions than when he was actually striking notes; so that it may not be too much to say that the attention of a first-rate player may have been exercised—to an infinitesimally small extent, but still truly exercised—on as many as ten thousand occasions within the space of five minutes, for no note can be struck nor point attended to without a certain amount of attention, no matter how rapidly or unconsciously given."

Sir James Paget has pointed out that in rapid piano-playing, of a master like Liszt or Paderewski, the finger moves 24 times a second, each movement involving at least three muscular contractions, which if multiplied by ten gives 720 impulses per second for both hands.

CHAPTER X

PRECOCITY AND GENIUS

*"Genius" (which means transcendent capacity of taking
trouble, first of all).*　　　　THOMAS CARLYLE.

THE author was brought up in the school in which little
boys were told they should be seen and not heard and,
perhaps as a result of that upbringing, he has always
evinced an instinctive dislike of the precocious child. But
the little chap may not be to blame for his prematurely
developed intellect; the responsibility probably lies with
his father, or his grandfather, so grandfathers beware!
Precocity is almost entirely confined to the masculine
gender—the precocious little girl is a thing unheard of and
unseen! And, despite the handicap under which he started
his career on this terrestrial globe, many a precocious
child has proved in later life to be a very modest genius.
We have already discovered many examples of precocity
among calculating boys, chess and musical prodigies.
Without great difficulty one could fill a book on the doings
of wonder children, but let us consider a few of the more
striking cases:

CHRISTIAN FRIEDRICH HEINECKEN, a German, who was
known as the "Infant of Lubeck", from the place where he
was born in 1721, is said to have talked within a few hours
after his birth. Besides his remarkable faculty for numbers,
he is said to have known, at the age of one year, all the
principal events related in the Pentateuch; at two was well
acquainted with the historical events of the Bible, and at

three had a knowledge of universal history and geography, Latin and French. People came from all parts to see him, and the King of Denmark had him brought to Copenhagen in 1724, in order to assure himself of the truth of what he had heard regarding him. But shortly after this, little Heinecken was taken ill and predicted his own death, which took place in 1725, at the tender age of four.

JEAN LOUIS CARDIAC, known as the "Wonder Child" was born, in 1719, at the Chateau de Cardiac, France. When three months old he could repeat the alphabet. At the age of three years he could read Latin and at four he could translate it either into French or English. He could read Greek and Hebrew at six and was proficient in the principles of arithmetic, history, geography and heraldry! He died, in Paris, at the age of seven.

WILLIAM JAMES SIDIS, another wonder child, this time from the United States, could read and write at two years of age; spoke French, Russian, English, German, with some Latin and Greek at eight and at eleven lectured on the fourth dimension to a gathering of professors. At 25 he was earning £5 a week in an office and he died at the age of 46.

KENNETH WOLF, at Cleveland, Ohio, could talk perfectly at four months, read at one year and matriculated when he was nine.

PAUL JOSEPH BARTHEZ, a famous French physician was born in 1734, and was included by Baillet among his *Enfants Célèbres* as being born to literature. At nine years of age he recited by heart all the comedies of Terence, without missing a line. The learned admired the prodigy, while the prodigy was writing books before he had a beard. He studied, without using references, trusting to his memory which is said to have been of amazing strength.

JEAN PHILLIPPE BARATIER died in 1740, when he was nineteen years old. At four years of age he could speak German, French and Latin; at five he translated the Greek bible: at six he was a member of an ecclesiastical synod in Berlin and also of the Royal Academy in the same city. He became a doctor of philosophy at 14.

Among our own countrymen, THOMAS BABINGTON MACAULAY must rank, not only as a precocious child but, later in life, as an all-round genius. At the age of seven he compiled a universal history; at eight he composed a treatise intended to convert the natives of Malabar to Christianity, and in his early teens he could recite the whole of *Paradise Lost*. He was a voracious reader and it is said that he could remember everything that he had ever read.

JOHN RUSKIN (1819–1900), author and art critic, was another British child prodigy who wrote poems at six and, as a small boy, was known as the "savant in petticoats". From his earliest years, he was compelled by his parents to practise the composition of both prose and verse.

JOHN STUART MILL (1806–1873), the philosopher economist, was even more remarkable. At three years of age he knew Greek; at six he could read Xenophon, Herodotus, Aesop and Lucian and at ten "with ease" he studied Plato and Demosthenes.

BLAISE PASCAL (1623–1662), a mathematical genius and author of one of the most profound religious books, was born at Clermont Ferrand on 19 June, 1623. His father was Etienne Pascal, president of the Court of Aids at Clermont.

His mother, who died when he was four years old, was named Antoinette Begon. This eminent mathematician, physicist and inventor was well taught by his father in languages and philosophy. Of good family, their home life was one of culture and fine manners and they were accustomed to the society of the noble and eminent. Father and son had much in common. When Pascal was about seven years old, his father gave up most of his official duties and devoted himself to the education of his children.

Great as is Pascal's reputation as a philosopher and man of letters, it may be fairly questioned whether his claim to be remembered by posterity as a mathematician and physicist is not even greater. He was a great mathematician in an age which produced Descartes, Fermat, Huyghens and Wallis. There are wonderful stories on record of his precocity in mathematical learning, which is sufficiently established by the well-attested fact that, before he was sixteen years of age, he had completed a work on conic sections. It is said that Descartes at first refused to believe that this was the work of a student and not that of a master. He wrote treatises on acoustics when only twelve years of age. When still a boy he became interested in the design of a calculating machine and completed the first machine, in 1643, when he was a youth of nineteen. It is stated that he was spurred on to the production of this machine by seeing when only a small boy, the burden of arithmetical labour involved in his father's official duties as supervisor of taxes at Rouen.

Whether we look at his pure mathematical or at his physical researches, we receive the same impression of Pascal. We see the evidence of a great original genius, creating new ideas, and seizing upon, mastering, and pursuing farther everything that was fresh and unfamiliar in his time. When thirty years of age, Pascal became attached to one of the stricter religious sects and lived the

life of a recluse. He died when he was thirty-nine years of
age and his biographers record some curious facts concerning his later life. It seems that on one occasion, when
he was driving to, Neuilly, the horses took fright and would
have plunged the carriage into a river had not the traces
fortunately broken. It is related that afterwards he was
constantly seeing an imaginary precipice at his bedside, or
at the foot of the chair on which he was sitting. From
23 November, 1654, dates the singular document, usually
known as "Pascal's Amulet", a parchment slip which he
wore constantly about him, and which bore the date followed
by some lines of a mystical nature.

Most calculators were precocious. GAUSS began his
calculations before he was three years old: AMPÈRE between
three and five; WHATELY at five; PUGLIESE and SUCCARO,
at about five; SAFFORD at six or earlier; MATTHIEU LE COQ,
MR. VAN. R., BIDDER, PROLONGEAU and INAUDI at six;
MONDEUX at seven; FERROL, MANGIAMELE, GRANDMANGE
and PIERINI, at early ages not definitely stated.

"Mathematical precocity," says Mitchell, "stands in a
class by itself, as a natural result of simplicity and isolation
of mental arithmetic. There is nothing wonderful or
incredible about it. The all-round prodigy like Ampère or
Sir William R. Hamilton, or Macaulay is possible only in
a cultured family where books are at hand and general
conditions favourable, and he must possess genuine mental
ability. The musical prodigy again—Mozart is the stock
instance—must come of a musical family, hear music and
have some chance to practise so that he cannot long hide
his light under a bushel. But the mathematical prodigy
requires neither the mental ability and cultured surroundings
of the one nor the external aids of the other. He may be an
all-round prodigy as well, like Gauss, Ampère and Safford;

it is not improbable that Bidder, under favourable conditions, would have developed into such an "infant phenomenon" but he may also come of the humblest family and be unable, even under the most favourable conditions, to develop average intelligence. He may proclaim himself to the world, almost at once, like the all-round or the musical prodigy, or keep his gift a secret for months or even years."

Perhaps the most noteworthy feature of all the cases to which reference has been made is that the ability shows itself at an early age as a natural consequence of a prodigious memory. As a result, these children were able to acquire and make use of stores of knowledge which, in the ordinary way, would necessitate months or even years of constant study. No great originality was evinced in regard to invention or design. Most of these children were simply repeating what they had already memorized. They had what has come to be known as a "photographic memory".

It has long been a trite expression that genius is akin to madness. Would it be equally commonplace to suggest that precocity may be due to an abnormal condition of certain glands? Let us see what Dr. Louis Berg (Bib. 30) has to say about it. ". . . Within normal limits, the thyroid may dominate the personality picture and produce a type which is seen in every-day life and which is compatible with normal existence. Thus, a slight excess of thyroid secretion may be considered favourable to an individual. It may produce a superior type who is above average in intelligence, capable of reaching emotional and intellectual heights, alert, cheerful and bright-eyed. . . . He will be high-strung, lean, temperamental; he will have a rapid pulse and will tend to develop heart and nervous disorders. If these individuals press their luck too far, they 'burn out.' Many artists and poets, such as Keats and Shelley, who .

have evidenced intense sensitiveness have been thyroid dominated.

". . . Too much cortin (cortin is the secretion of the cortex or outer part of the adrenal gland) in childhood, sometimes seen as being due to a tumour of the gland, hastens puberty. The author has seen a six-year old girl who looked thirteen; she had large breasts, menstruated and had the intellect of an adult. Also, a seven-year old boy, with a similar over-secretion became a miniature man in a few months. . . . Both these metamorphoses are due to the sudden pouring into the blood stream and the absorption of an excess of cortin. Maturity within weeks!

". . . There is some ground for the belief that genius is touched with madness, for the schizoid personality not only is found in the ranks of the supermen but occasionally actually helps them to become supermen. The scientist who withdraws from the world and absorbs himself in research, often makes epoch-making discoveries because he is able to concentrate upon his problems without social distraction. The poet, shy and sensitive and repelled by the vulgarity of the herd, transforms their ridicule and dislike of him into rhythms of startling beauty.

". . . Musical genius has often gone hand in hand with schizoid traits: the source of inspiration is found in fantasy and day-dreaming, which gives these 'queer ones' a 'lift' above the humdrum existence of the rabble and the monotony of the workaday world. Berlioz was an example of this queer genius. Political idealists and reformers are unable to get along with people in particular but love humanity and plan Utopian schemes to make this the best of all possible worlds.

"Religions and cults owe their origin to schizoids like Savonarola, Luther and Calvin, who were fundamentally stirred by a Messiah complex. The monastic, ascetic, and religious hermits of all times have often been schizoids to whom the *real* world has been repellent. The scholar and erudite, working in his study, the philosopher cloistered in Koenigsberg, the scientist absorbed in his laboratory, the mystic receiving the revelations of another world—these too are schizoids.

". . . Thoreau retreated from the world to Walden and formed his philosophy, Kant, cloistered in Koenigsberg, and Spinoza, grinding lenses in Amsterdam, found in solitude an appeasement of their thirst for an understanding of life. Pascal forswore science and retired to Abbey Port-Royal to write in solitude. . . . Hermits in the wood, sages in the desert and wanderers upon the ocean have detached themselves from life in order to learn its secret; schizoids all, they somehow maintained their sanity. But for the average individual, a morbid desire for seclusion is the first flush of the dawn that heralds schizophrenia."

Some ten or twelve years ago, the Faculty of Princeton University, U.S.A. was credited with having drawn up a list of ten names of men of all time who have done most to advance human knowledge. The names were: Socrates, Plato, Aristotle, Galileo, Leonardo, Pasteur, Shakespeare, Newton, Darwin and Einstein. No such list, of course, will please everybody; this particular one is open to the criticism that it does not include a musician.

THE NATURE OF GENIUS

According to popular notion, the genius learns without study, and knows without learning. He is eloquent without preparation; exact without calculation: and profound without reflection. While ordinary men toil for knowledge by reading, by comparison and by minute research, he is supposed to receive it as the mind receives dreams. "His mind," says Beecher, "is like a vast cathedral, through whose coloured windows the sunlight streams, painting the aisles with the varied colours of brilliant pictures."

The common idea of a genius is someone endowed with transcendent ability but this does not appear to agree with the classification employed by Francis Galton and Havelock Ellis, who based their records, to a great extent, on the space accorded to noted people in the *Dictionary of National Biography*. One important aspect these learned authors do emphasize is the frequency with which ability is associated with descent and the fact that certain characteristics cling to families. In fact, Galton set himself the task of proving, as he thought, that a man's natural abilities are derived almost entirely by inheritance, under exactly the same limitations as are the forms and physical features of the whole organic world. To a great extent, he anticipated the modern study of eugenics.

At the present day, we certainly do not consider that high ability is a proof of genius any more than we look upon genius as a proof of high all-round ability. Galton and Havelock Ellis do not appear to pay sufficient attention to education and environment. It is only to be expected that their enquiries into the lives of many "of the more select classes" should give a higher percentage of men of ability than would be the case by taking at random an equivalent number of every-day folk. Many a young man, several generations back, entered parliament at an early age and achieved distinction before he was 25 years old, but this can be explained by the fact that in those days politics and parliament were looked upon as a career more so than is the case at the present day.

GALTON ON GENIUS

Galton leaves us in little doubt that his opinion was that geniuses were born that way. They had no choice in the matter and simply had to be geniuses. This is what he says (Bib. 31):

"I believe that if the eminent men of any period had been changelings when babies, a very fair proportion of those who survived and retained their health up to fifty years of age, would, notwithstanding their altered circumstances, have equally risen to eminence. Thus—to take a strong case—it is incredible that any combination of circumstances, could have repressed Lord Broughton to the level of undistinguished mediocrity.

"If a man is gifted with vast intellectual ability, eagerness to work, and the power of working, I cannot comprehend how such a man should be suppressed. The world is always tormented with difficulties to be solved—struggling with ideas and feelings, to which it can give no adequate expression. If, then, there exists a man capable of solving those difficulties, or of giving a voice to those pent-up feelings, he is sure to be welcomed with universal acclamation. We may almost say that he has only to put his pen to paper, and the thing is done. I am here speaking of the very first-class men—prodigies—one in a million, or one in ten million, of whom numbers will be found in this volume, as specimens of hereditary genius."

A MODERN VIEW

The views of a modern psychologist (J. A. Hadfield, Bib. 27) do not greatly differ from those set forth by Galton, as witness:

"Temperamental characteristics may be supernormal, for there are men and women of outstanding personality whose abilities are beyond the average, largely the result of a healthy, strong and balanced physiological make-up. This outstanding general ability persists in some families, generation after generation, producing men and women

who would be successful in almost any walk of life, capable
in business, skilled in their profession and in politics,
natural-born leaders of their fellows. The war has produced such men and women who would make their mark
anywhere by the force of their personality.

"There are others who are supernormal in specific
qualities like the genius, whose extraordinary abilities are
constitutional and innate. The definition of genius as 'an
infinite capacity for taking trouble, first of all' (Carlyle), or
as 'one-third inspiration and two-thirds perspiration'
(Emerson) is precisely what genius is not! It may produce
an outstanding personality, but no man by hard work
alone can become a genius. The very point about a genius
is that he has the capacity to do these things without
correspondingly hard work: indeed, the name implies that
these capacities can only be accounted for by his 'genius'—
originally a kind of guardian spirit who is conceived as
accompanying him from the cradle to the grave.

"Genius is something inexplicable and unaccountable,
some gift we possess apart from any merit or effort of our
own, it is innate and not acquired. Geniuses are often
unbalanced because they are of the nature of 'sports' and
ill-adapted to the environment in which they are called
upon to live. Great artists are always abnormal, in the
strict sense, though not necessarily pathological, because
they perceive things in the world around them which
'normal' (in the sense of average) people do not see, as well
as having the capacity to give form to that vision which a
normal person has not."

The pathways of a genius are frequently beset with
many difficulties. This would appear to be the opinion of
Dr. Louis Berg when he says (Bib. 30): "It is common
knowledge that many geniuses have been maladjusted, and
the situation is not difficult to understand when we see
they are faced with constant and senseless demands to

subscribe to codes designed for their inferiors. Too often they have lived centuries ahead of their time and have suffered the malignant hate of the average man who suspects and dislikes any variant from mediocrity. Ironically, later generations usually recognize the genius scorned in his own time."

An attempt has been made to find an answer to the question: "What is a genius?" The reply to this question could not be put in simpler language than that employed by F. W. H. Myers, when he said "Genius—if that vaguely-used word is to receive anything like a psychological definition—should be regarded as a power of utilizing a wider range than other men can utilize of faculties to some degree innate in all".

CHAPTER XI

FAMOUS MEMORIZERS

I've a grand memory for forgetting, David.
R. L. STEVENSON.

IN modern medical and psychological text-books, the function of remembering is usually divided into three parts: registration, retention and recall.

Registration of the material to be remembered necessitates a certain amount of concentration. Thus, a maniac will tend to remember only those things that especially impress him. In unconsciousness, we are told, nothing can be registered, and in a semi-conscious state only partial recollection may occur.

Retention may be disturbed by various causes but such disturbance should only be assumed if it is certain that registration and recall are unaffected.

Recall, according to the specialists, may be either automatic or voluntary. In abnormal mental conditions it is quite feasible that the capacity for voluntary recall may be impaired whilst automatic recall may be almost perfect. These phenomena, it is claimed, may often be observed in normal individuals who are fatigued, or in the aged, and the disturbance is most marked in the effort to recall names. The ability to recall is facilitated by richness and rapidity of association. In consequence, slowness of association may make memory disturbances appear more severe than is really the case.

"Repression" may play an important part in determining which material cannot be recollected although this does not, of course, apply to all memory disturbances.

Total loss of memory, over a long period, is generally a hysterical symptom. A normal quality of remembering is that it tends to mould the past according to desire and to fill in defects in memory with facts which may have been there rather than with facts that are genuinely recollected. When there is a pathological loss of memory, the gap is often filled in with the most elaborate fabrications. Patients not infrequently get the sequence of past events all wrong. The problem of time perception is still very obscure.

That individuals differ markedly in the way they think and imagine was proved by Francis Galton. When he questioned people about their power of conjuring up mental pictures of things they had seen, some maintained that they could picture an object in their mind's eye as vividly as if it were in front of them. Many disclaimed any such power and found it difficult to believe that others possessed it.

In the achievements of calculating boys, the ability to memorize appears to have been restricted entirely to figures. If their ability had not been so restricted they might have become men of genius. It is by no means unusual to find in each individual considerable variation in the ability to remember different things.

The ability to remember figures, however, to an unusual degree, is not exclusive to calculating boys. As an example, consider the amazing ability of the famous John Wallis, the teacher of Sir Isaac Newton. This English mathematician was born on 23 November 1616, and died in 1703. He was one of the founders of the Royal Society. In a letter to Thomas Smith of Magdalene College (quoted in the *Spectator*, 1879, Vol. LII, *p.* 11) he writes:

"December 22nd 1669.—In a dark night, in bed, without pen, ink or paper, or anything equivalent, I did by memory extract the square root of

30000,00000,00000,00000,00000,00000,00000,00000

and did the next day commit it to writing." (*Note by the author:* the figures were grouped in fives, as indicated.)

"February 18th, 1670.—Johannes Georgius Pelshower giving me a visit, and desiring an example of the like, I did that night propose to myself, in the dark without help to my memory, a number in 55 places:

24681357910111214111315161820171921222426283023252729231

of which I extracted the square root in 27 places: 157103016871482805817152171 proxime, which numbers I did not commit to paper till he gave me another visit, March following, when I did from memory dictate them to him. Yours etc, John Wallis."

Reference has already been made to Shanks, an English mathematician who in 1873, determined the value of π to 707 decimal places. Dagbert, the French mentalist, claims to have memorized π to 707 places so he may have obtained his figures from this source. One cannot help feeling that to memorize endless strings of figures in this fashion seems an appalling waste of time and energy. It would be dangerous to make this observation to a "figure-fiend", however, in case he should retaliate by asking whether it was considered that the millions of hours that have been spent on crossword puzzles, chess and the like were not an even more appalling waste of time!

INHERITED ABILITY

It would be difficult to cite a more typical example of inherited ability than that of Macaulay, to whose prodigious memory reference has already been made (*p.* 137). He was able to recall pages and pages of hundreds of volumes, a knowledge of which he had acquired by simply reading them through once only.

His grandfather, the Rev. John Macaulay, was a minister who lived at Inverary. He was a most eloquent preacher and is mentioned in Dr. Johnson's *Tour*. Lord Macaulay's father, Zachary, the slave abolitionist, was also a very capable man and a lucid and rapid writer. Lord Macaulay's uncle, Colin Macaulay, was a famous general and the right-hand man of the Duke of Wellington, in his Indian campaigns. He governed for many years a large part of the Madras Presidency and in spite of his active life, was a first-rate scholar both in ancient and modern literature. He was constantly mentioned in contemporary literature as a wonder for his erudition and abilities. Another uncle—Aulay Macaulay—was a brilliant conversationalist and wrote much of value. He was tutor to Caroline of Brunswick but died in his prime. A cousin of Lord Macaulay was the Headmaster of Repton, and a good scholar. Many other relatives and descendants were famous men.

Other examples of hereditary influence are those of the father of Seneca, who had one of the greatest memories on record in ancient times, and Porson, the Greek scholar—what came to be known as the Porson memory was hereditary in his family.

EXCEPTIONAL MEMORIES

Seneca refers to a man who, after hearing a poet read a new poem, claimed it as his own, in proof of which he would repeat the poem from beginning to end, which was more than the author could do! Pascal is said never to have forgotten anything that he had ever known and read. Grotius, Leibnitz and Euler are also said to have been endowed with a similar power of memory.

Cyrus, it is stated, knew the name of every soldier in his army, and the Athenian, Themistocles, knew the name of every one of the twenty thousand inhabitants of Athens. In more recent days, Daniel Webster, the great American lawyer, was credited with knowing by heart, amongst other books, the whole of the Bible, all Shakespeare's plays and *Paradise Lost*. Until he reached his teens his memorizing ability was well below the average. The renowned South African statesman, General Smuts (1870–1950), as a child was far from being precocious in that he did not learn to read until he was twelve years of age. Whether this was a handicap or not would be difficult to prove since he eventually memorized the whole of the contents of his library of 5000 books and could give immediately chapter and verse references of any quoted passage.

Ripley, of "Believe it or not" fame, says that Elijah, the Gaon, one time Chief Rabbi of Lithuania, possessed such a wonderful memory that he never forgot a book once he had read it. Professor Graetz, the noted contemporary historian, stated that Elijah committed to memory some 2500 volumes. He knew these by heart and could quote any passage at will. This venerable scholar resided at Vilna, the ancient capital of Lithuania which, at the time, was the largest Jewish settlement in the world. Ripley says that his memory is revered to the present day by the Jews of Eastern Europe and his portrait is prominently displayed on the eastern wall of almost every orthodox dwelling.

Dr. Johnson, it is said. never forgot anything that he had seen, heard or read. Burke, Clarendon, Gibbon, Locke, Tillotson, were all distinguished for strength of memory.

In allusion to this subject, Sir W. Hamilton observed that for intellectual power of the highest order, none was distinguished above Grotius and Pascal both of whom forgot nothing they had ever read or thought.

Leibnitz and Euler were not less celebrated for their

intelligence than for their memory; and both could repeat the whole of the Aeneid. Donellus knew the Corpus Juris by heart, and yet he was one of the most profound and original speculators in jurisprudence. Ben Jonson tells us that he could repeat all that he had ever written, and whole books that he had read. Niebuhr, the historian, was not less distinguished for his memory than for his acuteness. In his youth he was employed in one of the public offices of Denmark. An account book having been destroyed by fire, he restored it by an effort of memory.

Dante was, perhaps, more than any man of his age, skilled in the learning of his times. He sustained, at the University of Paris, an argument against fourteen disputants. It is claimed that he was conqueror in all.

Many extraordinary things are related of James Crichton —surnamed the Admirable Crichton (1560–1585). He took his M.A. degree when he was 15. Whilst still a boy he could answer his professors in any of twelve languages. Before his 20th year he had gone through the whole circle of the sciences and was distinguished for his skill in singing and playing upon all sorts of instruments. In Paris, he disputed in Hebrew, Syriac, Arabic, Greek, Latin, Spanish, French, Italian, English, Dutch, Flemish and Slavonic and, what is more extraordinary, in either prose or verse. He was killed in a brawl.

THE VALUE OF CONCENTRATION

There appears to be considerable difference of opinion as to the value, or otherwise, of concentration as an aid to memory. A study of the statements and examples of calculators goes to show that concentration is not an important feature in their performances. By way of explaining the conflicting views for and against concentration, it would be fair to say that mental gymnastics of an automatic nature, such as the multiplication of two numbers, do not necessitate concentration. In fact, in such cases concentration might well be more of a hindrance than a help. A good car driver is one who eventually goes through all the actions of driving quite automatically. Like a good pianist, when he has become experienced, if he endeavours to think out the various processes as he goes along he will become confused. On the other hand, a creator—whether it be in music, poetry or science—must of necessity concentrate his whole attention on the occupation on which he is engaged.

Mental giants of the past have exercised this power of concentration to a degree which may appear marvellous. It is said of Socrates that he would frequently remain an entire day and night in the same attitude—absorbed in meditation. La Fontaine and Descartes experienced the same abstraction. Mercator, the celebrated geographer, found such delight in the progression of his studies that it was only with difficulty he could be persuaded to leave his maps for such mundane purposes as eating and sleeping.

In Cicero's *On Old Age*, Cato applauds Callus who, when he sat down to write in the morning, was surprised by the evening; and when he took up his pen in the evening was surprised by the appearance of the morning. It is said of Marini, the Italian poet, that when absorbed in revising his *Adonis*, he suffered his leg to be burnt for some time, without experiencing any sensation of discomfort. Poggio relates of Dante, that he indulged his meditations more strongly than any man he knew. When the first idea of the *Essay on the Arts and Sciences* overwhelmed the mind of Rousseau, his agitation was such as almost to approach a delirium. It is related that when he was questioned respecting the mental qualities which formed the peculiarity of his character he referred it entirely to the power he had acquired of continuous attention.

Writing of himself, Hamilton said: "Men give me some credit for genius. When I have a subject in hand, I study it profoundly. Day and night it is before me and I explore it in all its bearings. My mind becomes pervaded with it. People are pleased to call these efforts the fruits of genius. Genius is the fruit of labour and of thought."

It would seem that a perfect memory can be a mixed blessing. The famous Dr. Leyden could repeat correctly a long act of parliament, or any other similar document, after having once read it. On one occasion when congratulated by a friend on his remarkable power in this respect he maintained that instead of being an advantage his memory was often a source of much inconvenience. If he wished to recollect a particular point in anything which he had read, he could only do it by repeating to himself the whole, from the beginning, until he reached the point which he wished to recall.

All the arithmetical prodigies possessed a remarkable impressibility in that they were able to grasp large numbers of figures on only once seeing or hearing them. Dase's memory, in this respect, was remarkable: "Twelve figures being written down . . . he would just dip his eye on them, not allowing his glance to rest on them for more than half a second. He would then repeat them, backwards and forwards, and name any one, such as the ninth or the fourth, at command."

Perception must not be confused with concentration—the meaning can better be covered by the use of the colloquialism "quick on the uptake". This ability to grasp immediately any matter concerning figures is well illustrated by Buxton who would allow two people to propose different questions, one immediately after the other, and give each their respective answers, without the least confusion. He would also talk freely while working out his questions, as if it were no hindrance at all.

Again, "cramming" is not the same thing as concentration. It is much easier to learn something by going over it twice a day for a week than by reading it over fourteen times consecutively. Tests conducted by Dr. H. M. Johnson are said to have proved conclusively that the best time to memorize anything is just before going to sleep. According to *Popular Science Monthly* (Bib. 20), in the Johnson experiments "bedtime memorizers" scored consistently twenty to thirty per cent higher than the rest. Apparently, material that has just been memorized "sinks in" more effectively in the drowsy period before actual slumber. The benefit was lost, Dr. Johnson observed, if even as little as two hours intervened between the time of study and bedtime.

Condorcet related of himself, that, when engaged in some profound and obscure calculations, he was often obliged to leave them in an incomplete state, and retire to rest; and that the remaining steps, and the conclusion of his calculations, had more than once presented themselves in his dreams.

In further evidence of the ability of most calculators to do two things at once, reference may be made to Fuller (*see p.* 17) who would suffer interruptions without the least discomfort and then go on from where he had left off, if desired, giving any or all of the stages through which the calculation had passed.

Dirichlet, the mathematician, says that he "established the solution of one of the most difficult problems of the theory of numbers, with which he had for a long time striven in vain, in the Sistine Chapel in Rome, while listening to the Easter music".

INDIAN EXPERTS IN CONCENTRATION

The reader who would like to pursue the matter further is referred to a little book by Professor Ernest W. Wood

(Bib. 21). This book has an interesting chapter on the Memory men of India. It tells of an expert who did the following eleven things in his mind (at one time) and afterwards correctly repeated the whole:

1. Played a game of chess, without seeing the board.

2. Carried on a conversation upon various subjects.

3. Completed a Sanskrit verse from the first line given him.

4. Multiplied five figures by a multiplier of four figures.

5. Added a sum of three columns, each of eight rows of figures.

6. Committed to memory a Sanskrit verse of sixteen words—the words being given to him out of their order, and at the option of the tester.

7. Completed a "magic square" in which the separate sums in the several squares added to a total named, whether tried horizontally or vertically.

8. Without seeing a chess board, directed the movements of a knight so that it should make the circuit of the board within the outline of a horse traced on it, and enter no other squares than those.

9. Completed a second "magic square" with a different number from that in the above named.

10. Kept count of the strokes of a bell rung by a gentleman present.

11. Committed to memory two sentences of Spanish, given on the same system as No. 6.

Of even greater interest and importance, however, was an exhibition personally witnessed and vouched for by Professor Wood, in the State of Morvi in Kathiawar. In this case, the memory expert, Mr. Nathuram P. Shukla, remembered a hundred items. There was a large gathering of people, seated on carpets in a big hall. Twenty people were selected and seated directly in front of the pandit. He attended to each of the twenty people in turn, and went along the line five times. Several gave him sentences composed of five words, each person using a different language— Gujarati, English, Sanskrit, Persian, Hindi, Mahratti, French and Latin—and the words were given out of order. One sitter gave him moves in a game of chess. Two others gave him figures to be multiplied and added together. Another carried on little conversations with the pandit on various topics. Another struck a little bell a number of times on each round. There were calculations of dates, completion of short poems and other items. After a hundred points had been made, the pandit meditated for a little while; then answered questions relating to the items, and finally repeated the whole.

Professor Wood had the good fortune to obtain from the pandit details of the method of memory culture in vogue in his profession. Professor Wood is also of the opinion that anyone who cares to do so may, with comparative ease, perform many of the feats of the *Ashtavadhanis* with a reasonable amount of practice. Various suggestions and methods of training are given by Professor Wood in his book.

Professor T. H. Pear (Bib. 22) makes the following interesting remarks on the subject:

"Experiment upon memory has made it clear that, whatever the relation between rapidity of learning and permanence of retention may be, it is certainly not simple and inverse. Some of the talents which make it easy for a person to learn quickly also contribute to subsequent ease and precision of recall. In this case, as in many others, the sentence which most nearly expresses the truth is 'To him that hath, shall be given'. The suggestion that either quick learning or prompt recall must invariably be paid for by a lack of 'depth' betrays an inability to distinguish between the raw materials of thought and the finished article, and is probably dictated by sentimental factors."

"DATAS"

In June 1901, a fresh arrival in the entertainment world was the occasion of much speculation. The name of this new attraction was W. J. M. Bottle but it was as "Datas" that he rapidly became publicly known. As the name indicates, "Datas" specialized in dates. He claimed that the power of memorizing was a natural gift and in proof of this he expanded this power to such an extent that in the particular sphere of his operations he eventually reached a stage almost of infallibility.

"Datas" was born on 20 July, 1875, at Newnham, Kent, where his father kept a small shoe-maker's shop. As an infant, he was very delicate and was unable to walk until he reached his sixth birthday. It will be readily understood that the education of a young sickly child of poor working parents, who had a family of eleven to support, left much to be desired. By the time he had received sufficient schooling to enable him to read, the family removed to London and at the age of eleven "Datas" was working as a newspaper boy. Some eight months later he became a parcel boy at Lordship Lane station and remained there for three years. Then followed a short period as errand boy and in November, 1891, at the age of sixteen, he obtained employment at the Crystal Palace Gas Works. For a period of five years he was occupied in various ways at the gas works, eventually landing in the blacksmith's shop as a striker, for which he was paid twenty-four shillings a week.

From the time he was able to read, "Datas" began habitually to commit items of information to memory with the object of repeating them afterwards at leisure. From memorizing shopkeepers' names he got to cabbies' and policemen's numbers and then to reading Lloyd's newspaper. Writing of himself, "Datas" said: "Paper in hand, I would sit down on a little stool in a cosy corner by the fireside, and, my head resting against the chimney-piece, I would concentrate all my attention on the matter I wished to learn. I soon exhausted Lloyd's, and, though continuing to read it weekly, went further afield. A copy of Tussaud's calendar of events came into my possession. The mention of famous names therein whetted my appetite for works of history and adventure."

This process of acquiring information was carried on in the little spare time that was available and it would appear that "Datas" took particular care to ensure that each impression was sufficiently vivid to enable him to retain it indefinitely and to recall it at will. It was not until after he began his stage career that he knew anything of mnemonics but what he describes as "mental pictures" were undoubtedly of this nature, as witness: "Suppose I am asked the date of the Great Fire in London. I give the correct answer—1666— and immediately there rises before me a panoramic scene, as it were, of that calamity, from its start in Pudding Lane, to its finish in Pie Corner. The picture that is thus marvellously and so expeditiously drawn for me is one of my own fashioning entirely. The pencils are Nature's and the materials are the suggestions conveyed to the optical nerves by the facts hidden safely away in my mind. In what precise manner they act I know not. Suffice to say, I have the vision, and it materially assists me in narrating my version of the facts, acting as an all-powerful mentor. When in the future you are called upon to answer any questions, endeavour to call up at the same time some 'mind pictures', for you will find their help of immense value. Remember that failure is the result of a weak mental impression due in the first place to lack of concentration of thought on the subject matter you are endeavouring to commit to memory. Make up your mind always to create the strongest impression you are capable of creating and eventual success will not be wanting. To me, it is now all the same, whether it is a matter of trivial or great importance. Practice has enabled me to store and reproduce each fact, mentally and visually; with practice, lengthy and constant, you can do the same."

This .is how "Datas" described the events of a day in June, 1901, that launched him on the successful career of a memorizer: "I had been working on the night shift, from ten o'clock till six and reaching home about 6.30, I went to bed. By mid-day I was up again, had dinner, and then took a walk to the Crystal Palace where fate had much in store for me. While taking a little refreshment, I overheard two gentlemen discussing the date of the finish of the great Tichborne trial. Neither knew the correct date so I ventured to give this. Finding how surprised they were at my knowledge, I felt encouraged, and continued with a number of dates of events in English history, etc. Quite unnoticed by me, a third gentleman was a listener to our conversation and when I had finished my long string of dates, he quietly came up to me and put the momentous question: "Would you like to go upon the stage?" He then and there took me to the Standard Music Hall, Victoria, where I gave my first performance."

The new form of entertainment became an immediate success and "Datas" left the gas works for the stage. He travelled throughout the British Isles and eventually acquired a world-wide reputation. During his performances, many curious and unusual questions were put to him and it is said that only on rare occasions did he fail to give a correct or satisfactory answer. As in mnemonics, "Datas" claimed that what he described as the "law of association" was the only real help in memorizing. He goes on to say:

"One idea begets another; therefore, when memorizing one idea, kill two birds with one stone, and also memorize the corresponding idea. It may be that you will not at once discover the associated idea, or ideas. Here you will again perceive the necessity for a searching analysis of your subject-matter. Suppose you wish to remember the date of the opening of the first railway line in England. Instantly the figure of George Stephenson arises before you. You recall the date of his birth, etc., the year of the great financial railway bubble, the opening of the Mont Cenis and Simplon tunnels, the dates of notable collisions, etc. A host of things come to mind, the mine of recollection fired by the magic word 'railways'.

"Where you have ideas which are, so to speak, unconnected, it is essential that in order to commit them to memory successfully, you should establish an intermediary idea as a connecting link, an idea which although not directly associated with either one of the two ideas you wish to memorize, is nevertheless indirectly associated with both so that in remembering either, the link manifests itself which binds the two together. You wish to remember Newton— gravitation, the link is the word 'apple'. You say to yourself an apple falls from the tree to the ground; falling is an act of gravitation. Who watched a similar action and noted the result?—Newton. You also have an extra aid by reason of a certain sort of apple being named after the great scientist."

"Datas" insisted that all questions put to him should be brief and definite. His replies, whilst giving the dates asked for frequently included additional information associated with the replies. For example, if he were asked: "When was Big Ben set up at Westminster?" he would, in addition to the actual date include other items of interest concerning Westminster and Big Ben. The following is a selection from the many thousands of questions he was asked to answer:

When did Lord Beaconsfield make his maiden speech?
When was Rugby School founded?
When was the Isle of Man purchased?
When was an observatory built on the top of St. Paul's?
When was the magic lantern invented?
When was Elizabeth Gaunt burnt at Tyburn for treason?
When was the first cannon cast in England?
When was Alexander the Great born?
On what date was Queen Elizabeth crowned?
When did Nero set Rome on fire?
When was Aristotle born?
When was the first Prince of Wales created?
When did the Married Woman's Property Act come into operation?
When was the first stone of Blackfriars Bridge laid?
When did a steamship first cross the Atlantic?
When was Manchester first made a city?
What was the date of the first parachute descent in England?
When was the Metropolitan Railway opened?
When did the Glasgow Bank suspend payment?
When was Queen Anne's Bounty established?
When was Toronto University destroyed by fire?
When was Chambers' Journal first published?
Who was the first Jew to receive the honour of knighthood and when?
When was Kensal Green cemetery consecrated?
When was a duty imposed upon soap?
When did Captain Blood try to steal the Crown jewels?
When were Corinth and Carthage destroyed by the Romans?
When were top-hats invented?
When was the first theatre built?

It should be placed on record that when asked how he was able to remember dates so accurately, "Datas" would frequently claim that he had no idea how it was done. Nor could the usual arrangements obtaining at a music-hall be described as anywhere approaching "test conditions". When inviting questions in the ordinary way, these would be fired at him from various parts of the building so that, to some extent, he had a choice from which to make his selection or to ignore awkward questions. It is also quite possible that to increase the entertainment value of his show a "stooge" or "stooges" were employed. To such a question as "When was Kruger vaccinated?" his answer "On March 15, 1826— and it took in four places—is that right, sir?" scarcely ever failed to bring down the house. This does not affect the genuine nature of his gift of which there was no question.

On one occasion the Lord Chief Justice of England was an occupant of the stalls. He put three questions: "When was the *Utopia* wrecked?" "When were the Corn Laws repealed?" and "When did Mr. Low propose to put a tax on matches?" "Datas" did not know until afterwards who was his questioner. After his "turn", however, whilst in the dressing-room his Lordship visited him and congratulated him stating that the correct answer had been given to each of the three queries. On another occasion, Sir Edward Clarke put a series of difficult questions to which "Datas" gave the correct replies.

A lengthy notice in the *Evening News* said of him: "The dark, well-knit young man who is appearing under the nom du theatre of 'Datas' at the Palace is a human Haydn's Dictionary brought up to date. For six weeks he has answered, quick as thought, all sorts and kinds of questions on subjects of historical or public interest. He predicts nothing, but forgets nothing that he has ever heard or read. . . ."

"Datas" did not confine himself to a knowledge of world-wide events. His acquaintance with the local history of the towns he visited was equally thorough. When visiting a fresh town this was his procedure: "I would first visit the police headquarters, where I could generally obtain a great deal of information regarding famous crimes and criminals associated with the place, big accidents, and so forth. Then I proceeded to the fire station to learn all that I could about important fires that had occurred in the neighbourhood. The remainder of the time I would fill in by inspecting local cathedrals, churches, museums etc., from all of which I managed to extract a great deal of valuable information. A few hours spent in the manner described, used to suffice to give me all the history of the place I wished for."

LESLIE WELCH—THE MEMORY MAN

The nearest approach to "Datas" at the present day is the well-known memorizer, Leslie Welch—the Memory Man. The many thousands who have both heard him on the radio and seen him on the television screen have been impressed alike by his ability and modest bearing.

In his radio demonstrations, Mr. Welch has given many proofs of his phenomenal memory of sporting events and, it is said, he is equally at home in replying to questions of a geographical or historical nature. His responses to the questions set him are spontaneous and are frequently accompanied by many additional items of information. For example, if he was asked the name of the winner of the Eclipse Stakes in 1947, he would probably include in his reply the horses in the second and third places and the number of runners, etc.

On the rare occasions when he is caught napping his failure, as often as not, is due to the fact that the information sought was not of sufficient importance for him to memorize; e.g. if asked to name the billiards champion for Wales in 1923 he would promptly admit that he did not know the answer. When he could not give the reply he would ask the questioner for the necessary information and when this was forthcoming would say: "I shall know the answer next time!" This indicates that his registration and recollection are practically automatic. In following his procedure one gets the impression that all the information he has acquired has been neatly docketed in a card-index mind and that it is immediately available when it is wanted.

Mr. Welch was good enough to reply to a long list of questions, concerning his gift, put to him by the author. He was born in Edmonton, London, on 29 December, 1907, and, in due course, attended the Latymer Secondary School. Mathematics was one of his best subjects at school but he does not claim to have possessed any outstanding ability in that direction. There does not appear, in his case, to be any indication of extraordinary memorizing ability during childhood and adolescence, apart from the fact that over these periods he always knew that he had a good memory.

As already indicated, Mr. Welch appears to possess an automatic memory but he states that this applies mainly to those subjects in which he is interested. In his case, his memory is of considerable practical use, apart altogether from its entertainment value, because in addition to giving memory demonstrations he is the general manager of a weekly sporting review and it is part of his job to study all forms of sport.

His recollections are of an auditory nature. He does not employ mnemonics and does not claim to be able to do more than one thing at a time. There is no question of his making use of any magical "stunts", nor does telepathy play any part whatever in his exhibitions. So far as he is aware, Mr. Welch has no physical or psychological peculiarities. In fact, Mr. Welch is a very ordinary man with a very extraordinary memory. His answer to the question "How do you do it?" is "a well-trained memory, a genuine interest (this is most important) and an expert knowledge on the subject".

CHAPTER XII

HOW AN ACTOR REMEMBERS

Like a dull actor now, I have forgot my part, and I am out,
Even to a full disgrace.

CORIOLANUS, *Act* v, *iii.*

IN these days of specialized education, memory training, as such, plays little part in the daily school curriculum. It would probably be true to say, however, that all learning is part of the process of memory training. This does not apply to memory demonstrations with, or without, the help of mnemonics but to the acquirement of general knowledge. This acquirement of knowledge—learning—is memory training in the true sense of the term as opposed to the parrot-like repetition of words which have no real meaning to the persons employing them.

It has been suggested in some directions that the memorizing of a series of nonsense syllables, such as dib, dax, sib, sax, etc., is helpful for training purposes. It is not easy to agree with this suggestion in view of the difficulty in visualizing words that have no meaning. It would seem that the time would more profitably be spent in memorizing words that create vivid mental pictures.

There is an amazing diversity of opinion on the question of memory training. A distinguished British psychologist is very emphatic in stating that the notion that memory is a kind of faculty which can be improved by exercise, much as a muscle is strengthened by regular gymnastics, is "erroneous", "out of date" and "wholly misleading". On the other hand, a learned Doctor in the U.S.A. is equally emphatic in claiming that ". . . our memory, like a muscle in the human body, can be developed and strengthened by proper training". Ideas on the subject have materially altered during the last ten or twelve years but the fact of the matter is that our lack of knowledge is still so profound as to discourage a mere layman from making any attempt to summarize the present position. Both sides may be right. On the one hand, there is abundant evidence that many illiterate calculators possessed an amazing figure-memory. On the other hand, there is the undoubted evidence, forthcoming from actors and others similarly engaged, that memory is improved by practice. Another possibility, which does not necessarily conflict with either of the two just mentioned, is that we come into this world in possession of latent knowledge which, like instinct, has been acquired not by ourselves but by our ancestors and passed on to us at birth.

During the latter part of 1950, Sir Cyril Burt gave a series of radio talks on "The Study of the Mind". They deserve every commendation for the fact that they were delivered in simple language, intelligible to the most non-technical listener. An extract from the sixth of these eight talks, taken from *The Listener* of 7 December, 1950, reads:

"As a result of a long series of experimental researches, a great deal has now been discovered about the process of memorizing; and many popular ideas have been exploded. For example, it is commonly believed that if children were made to learn long lists of words, dates, figures, or lines of poetry—things which for them may be quite devoid of interest or meaning—the daily practice will improve their powers of retention. Memory is supposed to be a kind of faculty which can be strengthened by mental gymnastics, much as your arm muscles are strengthened by regular exercises with the dumb-bells. Experiments have shown that this is entirely misleading. Forming associations between one set of words cannot help you to form associations between another set of

words, any more than opening up a new railway line
from London to Liverpool makes it easier to get from
Bristol to York. Sheer retentiveness is an innate quality
given to each one of us at birth. It varies for different
materials and from one individual to another. But with
one and the same individual it remains fairly constant,
except for changes in health and age."

Let us leave the problem of memory training to the
psychologists and devote our attention to the methods
adopted by those practical memorizers—the actor and the
actress. Acting is a creative art and whilst the ability to
memorize is essential to the actor, if he is to be successful,
many other things are equally essential. Like an orator, he
has to follow the laws of modulation, accent and rhythm.
He has also to give his attention to the special laws of
dramatic delivery which vary in soliloquy and dialogue. The
desire to give expression to feelings and conceptions is
inseparable from human nature. Man expresses his thoughts
and emotions by gesture or by speech, or a combination
of both. It is, however, with the actor as a memorizer that
we are chiefly concerned in these pages. Enquiries made
by the author suggest that the average actor is partly a
visile and partly an audile. His script is visualized mentally
while, at the same time, by repeating this aloud he gets used
to hearing his own voice speaking the words.

The first thing an actor does when he receives his script
is to read it through, silently, several times. Then he reads
it through two or three times aloud. The next step is to
memorize it, a paragraph at a time, on each occasion going
back to the beginning until the whole has been got off by
heart. There are no short-cuts to memorizing and the time
taken to learn a part is, to a great extent, dependent upon
the ability of the actor. If he has one of the principal parts
his progress is more rapid if the script is issued to him in its

entirety. Unfortunately, stage managers, whether in the interest of economy or following established custom, are inclined to issue script to the actor with his own part complete and all the other parts severely abbreviated, even to the extent of giving only the last two or three words as a cue to the part he has to follow: thus—

"Tell me of all that has been done to her!"

" . . . my fault."

"No money must be spared to remedy this mistake"

" . . . alas!"

This method means that it takes the actor much longer to get the true relation of his own part to that played by his fellows. The position becomes even more difficult where cuts or interpolations are introduced to meet special emergencies.

In repertory, or where a fresh play is given each week, the Tuesday morning of the week before the play is given will be spent individually, in reading the part. On the Tuesday afternoon, a collective attempt will be made on the first act, reading from the script. On the Wednesday, the first act will be taken without the script and acts two and three will be read aloud. Thursday afternoon is devoted to learning act two. On the Friday morning, acts one and two are given without the book and act three is read aloud. By Friday afternoon, the actor is expected to have his part word-perfect.

Some managers do not believe in prompting, under any circumstances. If an actor forgets his lines it is just too bad for him and his fellows and he must get out of the difficulty by "gagging" until he gets going again. If a cut has taken place, it is unwise to attempt to go over the lost ground as this will probably involve the repetition of something that has gone before. It is said that provided an actor keeps talking and his fellow-actors help him out at the appropriate moment, the audience will not notice the cut. Prompting, however, is usually done from the wings and often by gesture instead of verbally. On the Continent the prompter is in a little box facing the stage.

In the *Atellane Fables* of Latin drama, the actors improvised their parts on the spur of the moment. Similar methods were frequently adopted by the travelling theatres in the melodrama of some sixty or seventy years ago. Since Elizabethan days when a plain draped stage served for every scene, whether it was Warwick castle or a cottage by the sea, and all the female parts were played by boys, the art has changed much.

In a television play, two or three weeks are devoted to learning the parts. Curiously enough, a "dry-up" is more likely to occur in a television play than when acting before a large audience.

AUTOMATIC DELIVERY

When once the actor has become thoroughly acquainted with his part it would appear that in many instances the delivery becomes purely automatic. The audience may be profoundly moved whilst the actor is wondering what he will have for supper! The appropriate gestures always precede the spoken word. As might be expected, some plays are much more difficult to memorize than others but it seems that the difficult scripts, when once they have been mastered, are much easier to recollect.

Almost without end are the anecdotes of actors and their little ways. It is related of Forbes-Robertson, that when he was playing in the *Passing of the Third Floor Back*, the part made him terribly nervous. He said that once or twice he had really forgotten what act he was in at the moment and, on coming to himself, had been amazed to find that his tongue was faithfully repeating the proper lines.

In the *News Chronicle* (February, 1950), Elizabeth Frank tells how stage stars, stepping suddenly into a new role, learn to master their lines:

"Time and again we read of actors and actresses stepping into important roles 'at a moment's notice' and we are suitably impressed, but I wonder how many realize what such a step entails. It is, of course, part of the actor's stock-in-trade to learn lines and remember them and the facility to do so comes with training and experience. Actors, like other people, have different kinds of memory and different methods of learning words.

Many of them learn 'photographically'—Leslie Henson for instance, remembers the look of the words on the printed page, and during early rehearsals he uses a kind of mental 'reading-out-loud' technique. He was word-perfect in the first act of his opening rehearsal, only a few hours after receiving the script. (*Note by author:* This refers to the leading role in *Harvey* which Leslie Henson was called upon to take at a few days' notice). Others learn their words by repeating them out aloud and remembering their sound. Blank verse is always easier to learn than prose because of the rhythm. On the other hand, a 'dry-up' is much more serious, for it takes considerable skill to 'improvise', say, the language of Shakespeare.

Parts which are full of short speeches are much harder for the actor to learn than those with long ones which, incidentally, impress playgoers much more. Short speeches mean far more 'cues' and, in modern plays, these often resemble one another.

Some of our greatest actors have been very slow 'studies'. Sir Herbert Tree, for instance, often forgot his words, though he was not afraid to tackle the longest stage role ever written—*Hamlet*. Lewis Waller, in contrast, could learn a part by reading it through once. Vivien

Leigh is a very quick 'study'. Her role in *A Street-car named Desire* is almost as long as *Hamlet* and she knew it all within a few days.

The most striking *tour de force* in the history of the theatre, came from W. J. Holloway, when a member of Henry Irving's company. One morning, the great man woke with a sore throat; by lunch-time he was speechless. Holloway learned the role of *King Lear*, including all the moves and 'business' and went on that evening, without forgetting a line."

It is far more helpful to consider practical applications of memory than to spend much time on theorizing. That is why so much space in this book is devoted to the opinions of other people—where such people are in a position to know what they are talking about.

Under the heading *Does an Actor Feel?* Richard Prentis, in *John O' London's Weekly*, 1 March, 1940, gives the following information:

". . . Somebody once asked Coquelin what he thought of, every night, when he was delivering the great speech in the last act of *Cyrano de Bergerac*. He answered: 'Usually, I think of something quite different!' A well-known English actor told me that, one night, he found, during the second act, that he had calculated with complete accuracy, his income tax for the year.

J. T. Grein once wrote me: 'A great Viennese actress, who was renowned for her powers as well as her eye to business, was on tour in Sardou's *La Tosca*. In the famous torture scene, she rose to great heights. After a public ovation, her manager rushed into her room to offer profuse congratulations. But she petulantly stopped his effusion and said: 'You dirty hound, you accounted for only six boxes though nine were full—-I counted them during the torture scene'.

And once, in a talk with the late Norman O'Neill
. . . he told me how during the last War he toured with
Réjane when she was giving her famous recital of the
war-poem *Carillon*, during which, every night, she would
be in floods of tears. One evening, he said to her: 'Madame,
I suppose this affects you deeply?' 'Not at all', she replied,
'I feel nothing'. O'Neill then asked: 'How do you cry,
then?' And Réjane answered: '*C'est mon métier!*'—It was
her job to cry—so she cried."

CHAPTER XIII

MNEMONICS

And the best and the worst of this is
That neither is most to blame,
If you have forgotten my kisses
And I have forgotten your name.
SWINBURNE.

THE word "mnemonics" is derived from a Greek word meaning "to remember", "call to mind" and is pronounced nee-mon-icks. It is probable that most of us, quite unconsciously in the majority of instances, have made extended use of mnemonics right from childhood days when we commenced our education by being taught that "A" stood for apple, "C" stood for cow. Even today, if we want to know how many days there are in June or July we repeat the familiar:

Thirty days hath September,
April, June and November,
All the rest have 31,
Excepting February alone,
Which has 28 days clear,
29 in each leap year.

Mnemonics are frequently referred to by Plato and Aristotle, and the Greek poet Simonides, who had a prodigious memory, is said to have been its inventor. The art was employed long before his time, however, both by civilized and partly-civilized peoples. Filton states that many of the North American tribes employed a set of mnemonic signs by means of which things once learned could be recalled to the memory.

Simonides's plan was based on local memory; he deposited thoughts in places and his system of associating ideas with the various parts of rooms and buildings became a favourite pastime with the Greeks and Romans. A similar system is employed today by many successful mentalists. Such systems are often described as an "artificial" aid to memory but in actual fact they are usually based on a natural association of ideas.

The art of mnemonics in Europe was revived by Gregor von Feinaigle of Baden, who lectured on the subject in France and England in 1807–1808 and published his system in 1812. This system is still in use for memorizing numbers and dates. For this purpose a code is formed on the following lines:

1	2	3	4	5	6	7	8	9	0
d	n	m	r	l	j	k	v	p	s

Each figure or digit should instantly suggest to the student the corresponding letter, as shown above. Vowels are freely inserted to devise a word that can easily be remembered. For example, if you wanted to remember a friend's telephone number, say, 5212, in the above system you would associate this friend with some such word as LoNDoN or LaNDiNg (L, N, D, N). Alternatively, discarding the Feinaigle system you could associate your friend with the word "year" or "time"; there are 52 weeks or 12 months in a year and having impressed that word on your mind you would automatically associate 52 and 12 with 5212.

The author, at one time, made use of a phonetic system —shorthand writers will perhaps recognize the association:

1	2	3	4	5	6	7	8	9	0
P.B.	T.D.	CH.J.	K.G.	F.V.	S.Z.	M.	L.	R.	N.

For figures 1 to 6 inclusive any one of two letters may be used. Arranged in three groups for figures 1 to 9 we get the words pitch, gives, molar. (PiTCH, GiVeS, MoLaR.) The following jingle may be of help in memorizing.

Letters P.B.   T.D.   Chay Jay
are numbers 1, 2, 3 we'll say:
Kay, Gay, eF, Vee, eS, Zee, we'll fix
For figures 4 and 5 and 6.
Let M and L and R define,
Figures 7 and 8 and 9,
And N will stand for nought.

The date 1950 with the above system would be covered
by the word "paraffin" (spelt phonetically—P a R a F i N).
If more convenient, the code could be used for the initial
letters of a sentence: thus, for 1950 we might employ
Policeman Rescues Four Nurses. Figures are more difficult
to memorize than objects but it is all a question of practice
and imagination.

AN AMAZING MEMORY DEMONSTRATION AND HOW TO DO IT

Many readers will have witnessed what appear to be
the amazing memory demonstrations of mentalists and
others. The author, in his magical days, was fond of giving
these demonstrations, which invariably elicited rounds of
applause—but it is all very simple.

A packet of cards—plain except that they are numbered
from 1 to 26—is handed out to members of the audience.
Those who possess these cards are then instructed to write
on them the name of any object they wish. The mentalist
next calls out the numbers from 1 to 26 and as each number
is called the person in the audience with the corresponding
card gives the name of the object he has written on this
card. For example, the mentalist might call "1" and the
owner of the card might say "cricket bat". The mentalist
repeats the word and then immediately calls for the next
number. When he comes to the last card the mentalist
immediately repeats backwards and then forwards the

numbers with the corresponding objects written on each card. He then invites members of the audience to call out any card number and immediately gives the name of the object written on the corresponding card. Alternatively, if a member of the audience prefers to call out the name of the object the mentalist gives the card number. As a proof that the names were indelibly impressed on his memory the mentalist may offer to name the objects a couple of hours later or even the next day, if desired.

This is how it is done—or rather, this is how it was done by the author. Methods may vary according to the whim of the performer but the basic idea is the same in most cases. He employed his own code covering numbers from 1 to 26—it could, of course, be extended to cover a greater number than 26 but this was quite long enough for the purpose for which it was intended.

The author gives the code exactly as he employed it. Some of the key-words were selected for personal reasons and it will be seen that in most cases there is some association between the number and the object:

   1 BARROW—a barrow has ONE wheel

   2 BED—a bed for two is visualized

   3 TREE—Rhyming association between "three" and "tree"

   4 DOOR—Rhyming association

   5 HIVE—Rhyming association

   6 DANCE FLOOR—Dances used to be described as SIXpenny hops

   7 SHOE—Size SEVEN

   8 SLATE—Rhyming association

   9 TABLE—Rhyming association between "nine" and "dine"—dining-table

  10 TENT—Spelling association

11 LOAF—LEVENED bread

12 SHELF—Rhyming association between "twelve" and "shelve"

13 BATH—13 is associated with luck—lucky dip—bath

14 MOTOR TRUCK—Rhyming association with FORD TIN Lizzie

15 TV SCREEN—TV and rhyming

16 BRICK WALL—Rhyming association between "six" and "bricks"

17 SOUP TUREEN—Rhyming association

18 18th GREEN—Golf association

19 19th HOLE—Bar—Golf association

20 £1 NOTE—Twenty shillings

21 BIG DRUM—21st Birthday—Beat the big drum!

22 CLOCK FACE—The time is TWENTY T(W)O

23 SEASHORE—Sands by the Sea—Rhyming association

24 GARAGE FLOOR—An empty garage—rhyming association

25 FRONT DRIVE—Rhyming and personal association

26 HAYRICK—Rhyming and personal association

Now each of the objects from 1 to 26 is visualized *in situ* exactly as it exists—and very vividly visualized too. The barrow is a particular barrow and the bed is in a certain room and so on. Each object will hold another object or consists of something on which a picture may be mentally impressed; for example, if item 22 is a fire-engine the mentalist imagines a vivid picture of a fire-engine pasted across a clock-face.

Now take a list of objects supposed to have been called out by various members of the audience.

1 SOAP—visualize a large bar of soap in a wheel-barrow

2 BANANA—A banana tucked in bed, with the stalk end on the pillow

3 FLAG—Union Jack flying merrily in the breeze at the top of a tree

4 SCISSORS—One point of the scissors stuck through the door

5 TOP-HAT—A top-hat on a bee-hive

6 UMBRELLA—An open umbrella in the middle of an empty dance floor

7 MUSTARD—Mustard smeared all over a shoe

8 ELEPHANT—An elephant drawn in chalk on a slate

9 AEROPLANE—A small aeroplane on a big table

10 DONKEY—A donkey tied to a tent pole

11 SWORD—A loaf stuck on the end of a sword

12 CANDLE—A lighted candle on a shelf

13 BOOK—An open book floating in a few inches of bath water

14 CIGARETTE—A giant cigarette in a motor-truck

15 CAT—A black cat filling a TV screen

16 EGG—Egg on a wall—humpty-dumpty

17 ROLLING PIN—A rolling pin in a soup tureen

18 DOLL'S HOUSE—A doll's house on the 18th green

19 BALLOON—A large toy balloon on the club-house bar

20 BUCKET—A bucketful of £1 notes

21 MONKEY—A monkey sitting on top of a drum

22 TABLE-CLOTH—A clock shrouded in a table-cloth

23 TRAIN—A train running on lines laid on a sandy shore

24 CONCERTINA—A concertina in the midst of an empty garage floor

25 APPLE TREE—An apple tree growing in the middle of a drive

26 PARACHUTE—A parachute entangled in a hayrick

The extraordinary thing about this memory business is that it really does work. If object No. 2 is say, a cow, once the cow has been tucked in bed there is no need to worry further about it and the mentalist can immediately get on to the next object. Of course, if he wants to gain a little time he can have an assistant to write down the names on a blackboard but it is much more impressive to go about it smartly and the more absurd the situation visualized the easier it is to remember. Curiously enough, the mentalist, if necessary, can give a second performance immediately after the first with an entirely fresh list of objects and he is able to keep them in proper sequence.

If the mentalist desires to demonstrate his ability to memorize a long string of figures he can employ the same system. In this case, No. 11 would be used for the first basic figure object, No. 12 for the next and so on. Suppose the figures to be memorized were 314159265. Place on or in the objects from No. 11 onwards the objects represented by objects 1 to 10. Thus, for the above number:

No. 11—LOAF	3 (tree) would be seen as a tree growing out of a loaf
No. 12—SHELF	1 (barrow) we should picture a little barrow on a shelf
No. 13—BATH	4 (door) a large door in a bath
No. 14—TRUCK	1 (barrow) a barrow in the middle of a motor truck
No. 15—TV SCREEN	5 (hive) a beehive filling a TV screen

No. 16—WALL	9 (dine) a dining-table on the top of a wall
No. 17—TUREEN	2 (bed) a soup tureen upset in a bed
No. 18—GREEN	6 (dance floor) a putting hole with flag in dance floor
No. 19—Bar	5 (hive) a beehive full of beer on the counter of a bar

It takes much longer to describe a tree growing out of a loaf than it does to visualize it but the reader who cares to try it out will, after a little practice, find the mental response will be immediate. The main essential is that the numbers with their corresponding objects should be so memorized that *immediately* one associates, say, 21 with a drum.

Whilst actually engaged on the preparation of this book for the press, the author had an entirely unexpected practical demonstration of the use of mnemonics as an aid to public speaking. Following a dinner, a visitor from overseas was called upon at short notice to respond to the toast of "The Visitors". In no way perturbed, the visitor, who was an Australian, was seen to arrange the objects on the table at which he was sitting (ash-tray, bottle, glass, matches, etc.) in some sort of order. As he dealt with the various points in his speech he moved the objects to one side. It was all done so naturally as not to be noticeable, in the ordinary way. On being approached afterwards, the speaker explained that the practice was often resorted to in his part of the world. Instead of making use of notes, the association of ideas was obtained from the simple objects on the table in front of him and he gave a very natural and impressive speech.

It is well-known that many public speakers (especially during election times!) make use of stock portions of previously delivered speeches, varying the arrangement to suit the audience. A speaker with a knowledge of mnemonics would readily associate various ideas with the objects visible to his sight, such as the ceiling, table, person next to him, windows, floor, doors, etc.

There is little doubt, however, that the best speeches are those which have been carefully prepared and memorized beforehand. This statement will probably evoke a cry of protest but the facts are that the most famous orators from Winston Churchill at the present day to the public orators of ancient times, repeated their speeches from memory. Of course, such speakers are alert to take advantage of "noises off" and interruptions and not to make too prominent a display of any notes. By carefully preparing and rehearsing the speech aloud beforehand a passage is provided through which the stream of eloquence may flow in a manner that cannot be bettered, and can rarely be equalled, by an extempore speaker.

What is known as Gematria has long been an accomplishment of Hebrew scholars and may be likened to mnemonics. It is a cabbalistic system of interpreting the Hebrew scriptures by interchanging words whose letters have the same numerical value when added. By means of this system the Talmudist is enabled to quote a series of numbers, which may run into hundreds, and to repeat exactly the same numbers and in the same order as often as required. This does not mean that he has memorized all these numbers. He has memorized passages of the Hebrew Scriptures and translated these into the language of Gematria. A mentalist would have little difficulty in giving a similar demonstration.

SECTION IV

MENTAL MAGIC

CHAPTER XIV

ARITHMETICAL PROBLEMS

Ah, but my computations, people say,
Reduced the year to better reckoning?—Nay,
'Twas only striking from the calendar
Unborn tomorrow and dead yesterday.

OMAR KHAYYAM.

In the introduction to this book, *p.* 12, reference was made to the close link between the effects produced by mental prodigies and those demonstrated by specialists in mental magic. The chief difference between a mentalist and a calculator is that the one solves his problems by deliberate concentrated mental effort whilst the other achieves his results, in much less time, with no conscious mental exertion. Constant practice on the part of the mentalist will reduce the gap between the two to the extent that certain magic routines, in course of time, become almost automatic.

This chapter will give the reader an insight into a few of the many arithmetical effects which, after some practice, may be performed mentally by anyone of average intelligence. Many of these methods have come to be known as "magical" because they have been fostered and developed by members of the magical fraternity for the entertainment and edification of the uninstructed. Most of the examples in this section, where the use of numbered cards is suggested, can equally well be performed with ordinary playing cards and vice versa.

At one time, the author devoted many months in the endeavour to discover some method of determining readily whether a given number was prime or not. Euler and Gauss attached great importance to this problem but failed to establish any conclusive test. There is considerable evidence to show that Fermat possessed some means of telling, from its form, whether a number was prime or not but, unfortunately, he left no indication of how this was done. Although the author's quest was without success he derived a great deal of pleasure from his figuring and came across many curious and interesting arithmetical problems.

Much of the information in this section was rediscovered by "fiddling with figures". The word "rediscovered" is used advisedly! From the days of Zeno, the ancient Greek philosopher who was born about 490 B.C., mathematicians have taken great delight in giving a magical twist to a simple arithmetical problem, with apparently miraculous results. It follows that most of these effects must have been known at some time or other although the adoption of figures to magical purposes is a little different. This Section may be likened to a sign-post, indicating the direction towards which the seeker desiring further knowledge should turn his attention. There is a vast literature on the subject and every week enterprising magicians are employing their knowledge of legerdemain to the introduction of new routines. Reference has already been made to two of the mystifying effects employed by Dagbert (*pp.* 62, 63) and these have rightly been described as calculating tricks. There is little doubt that most of the calculators, in course of time, became acquainted with various magical methods and made use of them for obvious purposes. Throughout this Section, the term "assistant" means a volunteer from the audience and not a performer's "stooge".

THE DAY FOR ANY DATE

One of the effects, favoured alike by calculating boys and mental magicians is to name the day of the week for any given date. There are many ways of doing this and most of those now in use are based on a formula given by Gauss. Methods which vary slightly from that given below will be found in *Rapid Calculations* (Bib 12) and *Mathematical Recreations* (Bib 17).

The author prefers his own method, probably because he is used to it and it cuts down the necessity for memorizing to the minimum. It is, however, necessary to memorize a special value or code for each month of the year, thus:

MONTH	MNEMONIC	VALUE
June	Juno	0
September, December	Septon, Decembon	1
April, July	Priltwo, Julytwo	2
January, October	Jantrois, Octrois	3
May	Mayfour	4
August	Augustive	5
Feb., March, Novr.	Febsic, Marsic, Novemsic	6

In leap years (last two figures of year divisible by four, without a remainder; the only exceptions to this rule are the century years 1800 and 1900; *see also p.* 187) January and February values are reduced by one. Setting out each month separately we get:

MONTH	VALUE	MONTH	VALUE	MONTH	VALUE
January	3	February	6	March	6
April	2	May	4	June	0
July	2	August	5	September	1
October	3	November	6	December	1

In leap years values for January and February reduced by one (*see above*).

Suppose the mentalist is asked to name the day for 5 October, 1888. If he is "in practice" he would immediately answer "Friday". This is how it is done—at first sight it seems complicated but once the routine has been mastered it is as simple as A, B, C.

5 October, 1888. Take the last two digits of the year (in this case 88); add a quarter (one fourth of 88 is 22) which makes the total so far 110, add the index for the month (October = 3) which brings our total to 113; add the day of the month (5) and we now have 118. Divide this number by seven and we get a remainder of 6. Counting Sunday as 1: Monday as 2: Tuesday as 3: Wednesday as 4: Thursday as 5: Friday as 6: Saturday as 0; we find that a remainder of 6 indicates Friday as "the day". It is the remainder, after dividing the total by seven, with which we are really concerned.

For the second example, suppose we want to know the day for 20 April, 1816. Following the procedure in the first example we get 16 plus 4 = 20, plus 2 (April value), plus 20 (day of the month) makes our total 42; divided by seven this leaves no remainder, 0 = Saturday; 20 April, 1816, fell on a Saturday.

When we have added the one-fourth to the last two digits of the year, we can divide by seven as we go along, as the final remainder will be the same. Thus, in the first example given above we can mentally divide 110 by seven and memorize the remainder of 5; to this 5 we add the October index of 3 and 5 for the fifth, so that our total is now 13. Divide this by seven and we have a remainder of 6—sixth day is Friday.

When the last two figures of the year cannot be divided by four exactly (to give the additional one-fourth) take the nearest lowest number divisible by four—in other words, ignore fractions so that for, say 1827 add six to 27 = 33.

To illustrate the last-mentioned point let us find the day for October 21, 1805. If we added exactly one-fourth we should make the number 6·25 but fractions are ignored so we call this 6. As 21 is exactly divisible by seven we can ignore this. The index for October is 3, 6 + 3 = 9 which when divided by 7 leaves a remainder of 2—so that 21 October, 1805, was a Monday.

The examples so far given have been concerned with the nineteenth century, *i.e.* 1801 to 1900. Where the dates occur in the twentieth century (1901 to 2000) we DEDUCT 2 from the final remainder. Where the date occurs in the eighteenth century, after 1752 (*i.e.* 1753 to 1799) we ADD 2 to the final remainder. Thus, if the year was 1911 and the final remainder was 2 we should deduct 2, leaving 0 so that the day would be a Saturday. For the year 1761 and a final remainder of 2 we should add 2 so that the day would be the fourth day = Thursday.

It will be noted that in this description we are concerned only with dates after 1752. The reason for this is that up to 1752 what was known as the Julian calendar was in force. In 1753, the Gregorian calendar came into operation. Under the Gregorian system the century years (*i.e.* 1800, 1900) are not leap years unless the first two digits make a number divisible by 4. Under this rule, the year 2000 will be a leap year and so will the year 2400 but not the century years between these dates.

In finding the day for dates prior to 1753 certain adjustments are necessary for which those who desire to pursue the matter further are referred to the two books mentioned earlier in this chapter.

Now let us find the day for a few dates in the twentieth century. 4 April, 1931 = 31 plus 7 (one-quarter) plus 2 (April) plus 4 = 44. Divided by 7 this gives a remainder of 2 but we have to deduct 2 for a twentieth century date so we are left with no remainder. 0 = Saturday.

12 March, 1937: 37 plus 9 plus 6 plus 12 = 64. 64 minus 2 = 62. 62 divided by 7 leaves remainder 6 =Friday.

8 January, 1900: 8 plus 3 = 11. 11 minus 2 = 9. 9 divided by 7 leaves a remainder of 2 = Monday. (*See note above regarding the year* 1900.)

21 October, 1906: 6 plus 1 plus 21 plus 3 = 31 minus 2 = 29 divided by 7 leaves remainder of 1 = Sunday.

To round off the examples let us take a date in the eighteenth century—say, 2 August, 1771. 71 plus 17 plus 5 plus 2 additional 2 for seventeenth century = 97. 97 divided by 7 leaves a remainder of 6 = Friday.

The reader will observe that the only part that calls for any effort in "the day for any date" is in remembering the month values. In this connection the use of mnemonics is strongly recommended.

SQUARING

There will be found elsewhere (*p.* 209) a simplified method of multiplication which will apply to the squaring of any number. For numbers up to, say, 25 however, the reader should have no difficulty in making the mental calculation in the ordinary way of arithmetic. For example, to square 16; to 160 we add 96 (6 × 16) and the answer 256 comes immediately into mind. Even where one is acquainted with the multiplication tables only to 12 times 12 this knowledge can be utilized for multiplying numbers much higher than 12. Taking a number at random—49—almost anyone can mentally multiply 7 × 7 × 7 × 7 and the answer = 2401 is immediately forthcoming. As this does not profess to be a text-book on arithmetic, suggestions have been limited to the squaring of numbers up to 100. The reader who would like to test his ability on larger numbers will find many examples in *Rapid Calculations* (Bib. 12) where we are told that a five-figure number should be squared mentally in not more than 30 seconds.

There are many mental short-cuts for the squaring of numbers up to 100 and some of the simplest of these are as follows:

To square any number from 25 to 50

Take the difference between the number and 25 for the hundreds and square the difference between the number and 50 for the tens and units.

For example, suppose the mentalist is asked to square 46. The difference between 25 and 46 is 21. The number 21 gives the first two figures. The difference between 50 and 46 is 4, which being squared equals 16. The number 16 gives the last two figures so the square of 46 is 2116.

This is all so simple that it is hardly necessary to give another example but let us now take 39. The difference between 25 and 39 is 14 which gives us the hundreds number; the difference between 39 and 50 is 11 which when squared gives 121. To 121 we add fourteen hundred and this gives 1521 = 39 squared.

To square any number from 50 to 100

Take *twice* the difference between the number and 50 for the hundreds and square the difference between the number and 100 for the tens and units.

For example, take 88. The difference between 88 and 50 is 38 which, when doubled equals 76. 88 from 100 leaves 12 which, when squared, gives 144; carry forward the hundred and we get 7744 which is correct.

EXTRACTION OF SQUARE ROOTS

The instantaneous extraction of a square root calls for a little more mental effort than the mere multiplication of two numbers. To ascertain the square root of any number that is the square of a two-figure number we must first of all memorize the square of each of the nine digits as follows:

Digit	1	2	3	4	5	6	7	8	9
Square	1	4	9	16	25	36	49	64	81

Suppose the square root of 3136 is asked for. In the first step strike out the last two figures and consider the 31. the number nearest to (but not greater than) 31 in the above table is 25 and the corresponding digit is 5; hence, 5 represents the first figure of the square root of 3136. The last digit of this number is a 6. There are two squares in the above table which terminate with a 6 and the number opposite one of them is the second figure of the root required.

The mentalist must learn to ascertain the right square number (the same thing happens when the square number ends with a 4 or a 9). We have discovered that the first figure of the square root is 5. Multiply this figure by itself = 25; deduct this from 31 (the first two figures of 3136) and 6 remains. This figure 6 is *larger* than the one we have multiplied (5); therefore select from the table above the *larger* of the two numbers terminating with 6 and the figure opposite the said number gives the second figure of the root (6), *i.e.* the root of 3136 is 56.

When the figure that is left after the multiplication and subtraction as above is *smaller* than the first figure of the root, the *smaller* square number is required in the table, ending with 4, 6 or 9 as the case may be.

The extraction of square roots is so frequently encountered in the problems solved by calculating boys that the would-be mentalist will find it well worth while to devote a little time to such calculations.

Here is a further example. What is the square root of 4624? The greatest square in 46 is 36, the root of which is 6. The difference between 46 and 36 is 10. 10 is greater than the root, 6; therefore the required root for the units must bu greater than 5. By the table it is seen to be 8; this is indicated by the unit 4 of the number. The required square root, therefore, is 68.

Third example: What is the square root of 6724? The greatest square in 67 is 64, the root of which is 8. The difference between 67 and 64 is 3; 3 is less than the root, 8, therefore, the required root in the units period must be less than 5. By the table it is seen to be 2—this is indicated by unit 4 of the number. The required square root, therefore, is 82. If the number of which it is desired to find the square root contains more than two periods (*i.e.* more than four figures), reduce to two periods by dividing by square numbers and multiplying the roots of divisors and the last root found together. The product will then be the required root. Example: What is the square root of 248,004? As this number contains more than two periods it must be reduced by dividing it by a square number. Divided by the square number 9 gives 27,556. As this number also contains more than two periods it must be divided by a square number. Divided by square number 4 gives the quotient 6889. In the tens period, 68, the greatest square is 64. The difference between 68 and 64 is 4. This difference being less than 8, the root of the units period will be less than 5; by the table it is seen to be 3, which is indicated by the unit 9 of the last quotient. The root of the last quotient (6889) is thus found to be 83 and this being multiplied by the roots 3 and 2 of the two divisors 9 and 4 will give the required root, *i.e.* $83 \times 3 \times 2 = 498$.

CUBING

To find the cube of any two-figure number it is helpful to become familiar with the cube numbers of the units 1 to 9, *i.e.* 1, 8, 27, 64, 125, 216, 343, 512, 729. It is really not necessary to commit these numbers to memory as it is a simple matter mentally to cube any number from 1 to 9 when it is wanted. Suppose we wish to find the cube of, say, 62. Put down the cube of 6 in thousands, to the left of the cube of 2, thus: 216,008 (6 cubed is 216 and 2 cubed is 8). Add to this the product of

62 × 6 × 2 × 3, *i.e.* 62 multiplied by 36 = 2232.

Place this under the first number moving the units figure one step to the left and add the two lines together, thus:

$$
\begin{array}{ll}
62 & 216,008 \\
& \underline{22\ 32} \quad (62 \times 6 \times 2 \times 3 = 2232) \\
& 238,328 = 62 \text{ cubed.}
\end{array}
$$

It only requires practice to perform these operations mentally.

Suppose we take a more difficult number, say, 99. This would be set out thus:

$$
\begin{array}{ll}
99 & 729,729 \\
& \underline{240,57} \quad (99 \times 9 \times 9 \times 3 = 24,057) \\
& 970,299 = 99 \text{ cubed.}
\end{array}
$$

In the above example it will be seen that for the second line of this little sum we multiply 99 × 9 × 9 × 3. If we wished to cube 54, the second line would be 54 × 5 × 4 × 3. If we were cubing 82, the second line would be 82 × 8 × 2 × 3 and so on.

Just a further example, say, 33 which should be done mentally

$$
\begin{array}{l}
27,027 \\
\underline{8\ 91} \\
35,937 = 33 \text{ cubed.}
\end{array}
$$

To cube a three-figure number is somewhat more involved than in the case of a two-figure number but to the mentalist who has become accustomed to the routine it calls for no great mental effort.

EXTRACTION OF CUBE ROOTS

It may be interesting to the would-be mentalist to know how to give instantaneously the cube root of any number, that is the cube of a two-figure number. To do this we must keep in mind the third power of each of the digits from 1 to 9:

Digit	1	2	3	4	5	6	7	8	9
Cube	1	8	27	64	125	216	343	512	729

and the tens from 10 to 90 (*i.e.* 1000, 8000, 27,000, 64,000, 125,000, 216,000, 343,000, 512,000, 729,000).

The mentalist distributes some slips of paper and requests several persons, in rotation, to select any number of two figures and to raise the said number to its cubic or third power. Suppose the number 72 is chosen; 72 × 72 × 72 equals 373,248 and it is, of course, this last number only (in this example 373,248) that should be communicated to the mentalist who writes it upon a blackboard. The mentalist now erases, *in his mind*, the last three figures (248) and considers the first three (373). He now, *also in his mind*, looks for the cubic number among the digits 1 to 9 which is nearest to 373 but not exceeding it. Such a number is 343 for digit 7. This 7 is the first figure of the root he requires. He further observes that the last digit of 373,248 is 8. Referring back to his digit values he remembers that the only number ending in 8 is the cube of 2. This figure 2 is the second digit of the root: therefore, the cube root of 373,248 is 72.

The method of mentally finding the cube root of a perfect cube has often caused surprise to many and can frequently be used to advantage. The cube root of any number of more than six figures must be over 100: if six figures, or less, the root will be less than 100. Example: What is the cube root of 804,357? At a glance it is seen that there are only six figures in the cube so the root will be less than 100. Again, the unit figure of the cube is 7 and on referring to the table it is seen that 3 is the only cube that gives 7 for the unit, and as 804 is more than 729 (the cube of 9) the answer will be 93.

Just one further example: What is the cube root of 314,432? The unit 2 in the cube shows that 8 is the unit in the root, and as 314 (in thousands) is less than 343 but greater than 216, the answer must be 68.

MEMORY TESTS

If the reader desires to demonstrate that he has a good memory and is an expert arithmetician, he can do so with the minimum of mental effort. A packet of cards is handed out to the audience. Each card has a small index number and a number of six figures in much larger lettering. All the numbers are different. On the back of the card may be written an amount in pounds, shillings and pence. Members of the audience call out the small index number and the mentalist immediately calls back the large number and the amount. Alternatively, by being given the large number or amount the mentalist can call back at once the index number on the card.

With a little practice, the mental effort required to perform this effect becomes purely automatic. In his early magical days, the author prepared a set of cards as follows: add six to the index number and reverse the number for the first two figures, take away six from the index number for the second two figures, take the units figure resulting from the addition of the first two figures for the fifth figure, take the units figure resulting from the addition of the second two figures for the sixth and last figure.

This all sounds very complicated but it is really extremely simple. The author has not demonstrated this effect for many years, but he knows immediately that the number accompanying, say, index No. 23 is 921,718, *i.e.* 23 + 6 = 29 which, when reversed, gives the first two figures = 92. 6 from 23 leaves 17, we now have 9217; the units figure resulting from the addition of 9 and 2 is 1—92,171 and the figure resulting from the addition of 7 and 1 is 8 = 921,718. When the procedure has been grasped these simple mental processes can be performed instantaneously.

One more example:

55 index = 164,973, *i.e.* 55 + 6 = 61 which, when reversed = 16 (first two figures); 6 from 55 = 49 (second two figures); the units figure resulting from the addition of 1 and 6 = 7 (fifth figure) and the units figure resulting from the addition of 9 and 4 = 3 (sixth figure). In this system 10 should be the lowest index number employed.

If it is desired to incorporate sums of money in the answers, it is suggested that figure 3 be added to the index number which should then be reversed for the pounds; for the shillings, cross-total the two figures of the index; for the pence, take the difference between the two index figures; for farthings, add $\frac{1}{4}$d. if the pence come to 4d. or under; $\frac{1}{2}$d. for 8d. down to 5d. and $\frac{3}{4}$d. for 1/– down to 9d. Thus, with the index number 23, employing this method the amount would be £62 5s. 1$\frac{1}{4}$d.

Perhaps, even more suggestive of a memory feat is the effect that follows:

MAGIC DIVINATION

From time to time, during the last century or so, what are described as Magic Age Cards have occasioned a certain amount of interest and amusement. The usual procedure is to employ six cards bearing 32 numbers on each. The person whose age it is desired to ascertain is requested to place on one side the cards showing his age. A glance at these cards immediately reveals the required information. There is another method, however, which is simpler and more ingenious in that the mentalist performing the trick does not have to see the cards.

Set out a table of twelve columns as shown.

COLUMN NUMBER	1	2	4	8	16	32	1	2	4	8	16	32
	1	2	4	8	16	32	33	34	36	40	48	48
	3	3	5	9	17	33	35	35	37	41	49	49
	5	6	6	10	18	34	37	38	38	42	50	50
	7	7	7	11	19	35	39	39	39	43	51	51
	9	10	12	12	20	36	41	42	44	44	52	52
	11	11	13	13	21	37	43	43	45	45	53	53
	13	14	14	14	22	38	45	46	46	46	54	54
	15	15	15	15	23	39	47	47	47	47	55	55
	17	18	20	24	24	40	49	50	52	56	56	56
	19	19	21	25	25	41	51	51	53	57	57	57
	21	22	22	26	26	42	53	54	54	58	58	58
	23	23	23	27	27	43	55	55	55	59	59	59
	25	26	28	28	28	44	57	58	60	60	60	60
	27	27	29	29	29	45	59	59	61	61	61	61
	29	30	30	30	30	46	61	62	62	62	62	62
	31	31	31	31	31	47	63	63	63	63	63	63

If a person says his age is in columns, 1, 2, 4, 8, 32 you can tell him immediately, without looking at the table, that his age is 47, you simply add 1 + 2 + 4 + 8 + 32. If he thinks of number 23 and tells you that the number thought of is in columns 1, 2, 4, 16 then $1 + 2 + 4 + 16 = 23$. The tables are numerically arranged and can be set in six long columns, if desired. The effect can be improved by numbering the cards 1–6, and memorizing the code number relating to each. A further obvious improvement would be to employ six cards of different colours which would reveal at a single glance the desired number.

Professor A. C. Aitken gives an easy explanation of the Magic Age cards. Every number can be expressed in one way, and in one way only, in terms of the powers of 2, namely, 1, 2, 4, 8, 16, 32 and so on. For example, $43 = 32 + 8 + 2 + 1$. All that the cards do is to make lists, in columns, of the numbers that contain in this representation the power of 2 placed at the head of the column.

CHAPTER XV

MORE PROBLEMS AND SOLUTIONS

I have often admired the mystical way of Pythagoras,
and the secret magic of numbers.
                                    SIR THOMAS BROWNE.

THE reader who feels so inclined should have no difficulty in developing the effects which follow into more intricate problems and, possibly, by giving them an original twist, to make them more entertaining. We will begin with a description of an ancient problem set by C. C. Bachet as long ago as 1612. A development of this effect will be found in the examples demonstrated by Dagbert (*pp.* 63, 64).

BACHET'S THINK OF A NUMBER

Ask a member of your audience to think of any number less than 60. Request him to divide this number by 3, 4 and 5 respectively and tell you the remainder in each instance. As soon as you know these remainders then you should be able to tell your victim the number of which he thought.

Solution: Suppose the number thought of was 58; this number when divided by 3 has a remainder of 1; divided by 4, it gives a remainder of 2 and divided by 5, the remainder is 3. These remainders are multiplied by 40, 45 and 36 respectively and the three sums are then added together. Thus, $40 \times 1 = 40$ plus (45×2) 90 plus (36×3) 108 gives a total of 238. The mentalist divides this number by sixty and the remainder 58 is the number thought of. The mathematical explanation of this method is given in Appendix II.

THINK OF A CARD

This is another ancient problem taken from an old book on Philosophical Recreations—"Several different cards being fixed by different Persons, to name that on which each person fixed".

Solution: To simplify this effect we will suppose that "A" is handed three cards, numbered 1, 2, 3. To "B" we hand three cards numbered 4, 5 and 6 and to "C" we give three cards numbered 7, 8 and 9. "A", "B" and "C" are each instructed to think of one card in their particular group. Suppose "A" thinks of 1, "B" of 5 and "C" thinks of 9. The performer takes the three cards from "A" and places them in three separate groups, face upwards, thus 3, 2, 1 (the order in which they are placed makes no difference) at the same time instructing "A" to note the group containing his card. The same instructions are given to "B" and one of each of his cards is included in each group. Similarly with "C". Suppose the arrangement is:

Group No. 1	Group No. 2	Group No. 3
1	3	2
4	6	5
7	9	8

Ask "A" to tell you what group contains the card he thought of. It will, of course, be the first card at the bottom of the pack; ask "B" to indicate the group containing his card, it will always be the second card from the bottom of the pack, whilst the card that "C" thought of will always be at the top of the pack. The description concludes "This Amusement may be performed with a Single Person by letting him fix on three, four or more cards. In this case you must show him as many parcels as he is to chose cards, and every parcel must consist of that number, out of which he is to fix on one. You then proceed as before, he telling you the parcel that contains each of his cards."

ANOTHER CARD DIVINATION

The mentalist hands a pack of cards to a member of the audience and instructs him to shuffle them. He next tells him to look at any card between the first and the tenth from the face of the pack and to make a note of its position. The pack is returned to the mentalist who takes the cards behind his back and volunteers the information that he has moved the chosen card to number fifteen in the pack. He asks the assistant to name the original position of the card and, beginning with that number, he counts off the cards aloud until he comes to "fifteen" which will be the card chosen.

Solution: With the cards behind his back, the mentalist transfers 15 cards (in the same order) from the face to the back of the pack. With the backs uppermost he counts off, beginning at the number given and the fifteenth card is bound to be the one selected. Thus, if the card originally selected was the eighth from the face, the mentalist, commencing with the top card, counts eight, nine, ten, eleven, twelve, thirteen, fourteen fifteen—exposing the face of the fifteenth card as he counts to show that it was the one selected.

A LOAN AND A PRESENT

This is an adaptation of an old problem by the late Professor Hoffmann, of magical fame.

The mentalist requests someone to think of a given number of shillings, large or small as he pleases. He is then, in imagination, to borrow the same amount from some member of the audience and add it to the original amount which of course, will now be doubled. "Now please suppose," says the mentalist, "that I make you a present of fourteen shillings and add that also to the original amount and the amount you have borrowed. Now give half the total amount to the poor: next, return the borrowed money and tell the audience how much you have remaining." The reply will be "Seven". The mentalist opens his hand and shows that it contains exactly seven shillings.

Suppose a member of the audience thinks of 16 shillings. He mentally borrows a similar sum from another member of the audience which, with the 14 shillings from the mentalist, now makes his total 46 shillings. He mentally gives 23 shillings to the poor, leaving him with a similar amount. Of the 23 shillings he now has, he pays back the 16 shillings that he borrowed, leaving him finally with 7 shillings.

In every case, the sum remaining in hand will be exactly half that presented by the mentalist.

GUESSING TWO CARDS

A packet of cards, numbered 1 to 20, is handed to a member of the audience and he is requested to think of any two consecutive cards, starting with an odd number. When this has been done, the pack is returned to the mentalist who lays out the cards in four rows. The assistant is instructed to denote the row, or rows, in which the two cards appear and the mentalist immediately reveals what they are.

Solution: The cards should be arranged beforehand in alternate odd and even numbers as follows: 1, 2, 17, 14, 9, 6, 15, 8, 19, 16, 13, 4, 7, 12, 3, 10, 5, 20, 11, 18. When laying out the cards in four rows, the mentalist places them according to plan over an invisible code. The classical code, used by the mathematicians of old, consisted of the words MUTUS, DEDIT, NOMEN, COCIS. A later code, of which the origin is unknown, is DAVID LOVEL IN YON ABBEY. Whichever code is used, each pair of cards goes on each pair of similar letters: for example, in the first pair of numbers 1, 2; 1 will go on "D" and 2 also on the other "D". It is immaterial how the cards are arranged provided they are kept in pairs (odd and even), and each card of each pair goes on the same letter. With the cards arranged as above suggested, their position on the table, using the "David Lovel" code would be:

D	A	V	I	D
1	17	9	15	2
L	O	V	E	L
19	13	6	7	16
I	N	Y	O	N
8	3	5	4	10
A	B	B	E	Y
14	11	18	12	20

Suppose cards 7 and 12 were thought of. The spectator indicates that the cards selected are in the second and fourth rows, horizontally. The mentalist knows from his code that "E" is the only letter common to both rows so that the figures must be 7 and 12. If the second row is indicated as containing both numbers then those numbers must be 19 and 16.

PUT AND TAKE

Invite a spectator to take any quantity of counters from a bag and place them in two unequal heaps. The mentalist, who has his back to the table, then asks the spectator to tell him the difference in number between the two lots of counters. He next requests the spectator to take a certain number of counters from the smaller heap. The counters now remaining in this smaller pile, together with an equal number of counters from the larger pile are, at this stage, placed back in the bag. The mentalist then states the number of counters remaining on the table.

Solution: Let us designate the small pile *S* and the large pile *L*. Suppose that *S* contains 14 counters and that *L* contains 20. The difference in quantity between the two heaps is, of course, 6. It is necessary for the mentalist to know this difference. Now instruct the spectator to take, say, 5 counters from *S*. There will now be 9 counters in pile *S* and 20 in *L*. The 9 counters in *S* and a similar quantity from *L* are placed back in the bag. In other words, 11 counters are left in pile *L*. This number represents the difference between the two heaps to start with (6) plus the number deducted from *S* according to the instructions given by the mentalist.

BIRTHDAY TRICK

Mr. R. Vale Heath, an American mentalist, in his excellent book entitled *Mathemagic* (Bib. 14) gives a good example of a birthday trick. This is designed to reveal not only the year of birth but the month and the day of the month also. The spectator is instructed:

1 To write down the number of the month in which he was born, counting January as 1

2 To add to it the next higher number in sequence

3 To multiply the figure thus obtained by 5

4 To add a nought to the right of his total

5 To add any number under 100. (This number must be mentioned aloud.)

6 To add the date of the month in which he was born

7 To place to the right of the sum obtained any number less than 100. (This number must be given to the mentalist.)

8 To add the last two figures of the year of birth.

The mentalist is advised of the total figure resulting from the above operations. He then adds 50 to the number given in step No. 5 and to the sum thus obtained adds to the right the number mentioned in step No. 7. The resulting total is then deducted from the sum submitted by the spectator and the difference reveals the required month, day and year.

Suppose the date is 12 February, 1899. In accordance with the above, the steps will be as follows: $2 + 3 = 5$: $5 \times 5 = 25$: o to the right $= 250$: $250 + $ (say) $32 = 282$: $282 + 12$ (day of month) $= 294$: $294 + $ (say) 22 (Step No. 7—any two figure number added to the right) $= 29422$: $29,422 + 99$ (last two figures of year of birth) $= 29,521$. From this total must be deducted 50, plus the number referred to in step No. 5, *i.e.* $32 = 82$, plus the two figures to the right given in step No. 7, *i.e.* 22 making the total deduction 8222. When this is subtracted from the total of 29,521, the resulting answer (21,299) indicates the 2nd month and the 12th day of the year (18)99.

When this is done, step by step, it is much simpler than it reads. All that the mentalist has to keep in mind (apart from dictating the stages) is to add 50 to the number introduced in step No. 5 and to place to the right the number introduced in step No. 7. The sum thus obtained is deducted from the total submitted by the spectator who has, of course, employed pencil and paper for his part of the experiment.

It is worth spending a little time in getting accustomed to the procedure in this very puzzling effect. Suppose the date to be revealed by the mentalist is 5 October, 1920, and say that the number introduced by the spectator in step No. 5 is 87 and that in step No. 7 is 78. This means that the mentalist will have to subtract 13,778 from the spectator's final total. This last mentioned figure is obtained by adding 50 to $87 = 137$ and by placing 78 to the right of this number

= 13,778. The spectator's sum will be: 10 + 11 = 21; 21 × 5 = 105; 105 plus 0 to the right = 1050: 1050 + (say) 87 = 1137; 1137 + 5 (day of month) = 1142; 78 (say) to the right of this number = 114,278; 114,278 + 20 (last two figures of year) = spectator's final total of 114,298. From this, the mentalist now subtracts 13,778, as above. The resulting number = 100,520 indicates that the date selected was the 10th month (October), 5th day of the month of the year (19)20.

DICE TRICK

A spectator from the audience secretly throws three numbers which are revealed by the mentalist upon being told of the following little sum. Suppose the numbers thrown to be 2, 6 and 3. The spectator is told to double the first number (2 × 2 = 4) add 5 (4 + 5 = 9); multiply by 5 (9 × 5 = 45); add the second number (45 + 6 = 51); multiply by 10 (51 × 10 = 510); add the third number (510 + 3 = 513); take away 250 (513 − 250 = 263). Spectator reveals the total 263 which gives the three numbers originally thrown (or thought of) in their correct order. The reader who may feel so inclined will experience little difficulty in disguising and elaborating this effect.

CHAPTER XVI

LIGHTNING CALCULATIONS

It must be done like lightning!
BEN JONSON.

A GENERATION ago, an essential qualification for an office vacancy was that the applicant should be "quick at figures". The arithmetical short-cuts in this chapter have been taken from a store accumulated during some forty years of accountancy and office experience. Some of the time-saving methods here described may be original. Others have been extracted from old records. The examples that follow bear a close resemblance to many of the problems submitted to calculators and may help to cultivate that habit of mental alertness which is the aim of mentalist and calculator alike.

The author has found that the digit 8, in connection with hundreds and thousands, plays a prominent part in British measures. A knowledge of these various combinations will enable the reader to perform what, to the uninitiated, appear to be intricate computations. The following methods will be helpful to those who wish to entertain their friends with an exhibition of lightning calculations. If a blackboard is available all the better.

GUINEAS TO FARTHINGS

The mentalist asks members of his audience for a three-figure number. Suppose someone gives the number 628. This number is written on the blackboard. Facing the audience the mentalist then gives the unnecessary information that there are four farthings in a penny; that twelve pence make a shilling and that twenty shillings make a pound. He next says: "To make it a little more complicated we will call these guineas." He then writes the word "guineas" after the number 628 and without hesitation, as rapidly as he can write down the figures " = 633,024 farthings". There are 1008 farthings in a guinea. In 628 guineas there will be 628,000 farthings plus 628 multiplied by eight. In other words, as he is writing down the figures, the performer mentally multiplies the number by eight; writes down the last three figures and adds the carry-over figure to the original number. After two or three examples the mentalist proceeds to prove one or more of his results by working out the sum at length, *i.e.* by writing the number of guineas on the blackboard and multiplying successively by 21, 12 and 4.

YARDS TO BARLEYCORNS

Three barleycorns make one inch; twelve inches make one foot etc. Very few people realize that 108 barleycorns make one yard. We can utilize this knowledge in a manner similar to that referred to in the previous example. Suppose someone calls out 367; the mentalist immediately writes this on the blackboard and adds ". . . yards = 39,636 barleycorns". Remember that in this instance the multiplier is 108 and not 1008. Prove one of your results by working out at length.

WEEKS TO MINUTES

There are 10,080 minutes in a week. Add a zero and treat the number just the same as you would do in reducing guineas to farthings, *e.g.* 84 weeks = 846,720 minutes. Prove one of the results by working at length.

GROSSES TO UNITS

Seven gross equals 1008. In making use of this information the mentalist might like to try a little variation from the examples cited above. Suppose someone calls out the number 365. Divide this number mentally by seven (*i.e.* 52, ignoring the remainder of 1). Write down immediately " = 52,416" (52 × 1008). Face the audience, then glance quickly at the blackboard and say "Sorry! I have made a mistake—144 goes into 52,416 only 364 times; I am one gross short". Alter the 365 to read 364 and then write immediately underneath "365 gross = 52,560" (52,416 plus 144). This little subterfuge is helpful in that we are dealing with seven gross lots and seven will not divide into 365 without a remainder. It will go 52 times into 364 without a remainder, however, so you proceed to multiply 52 × 1008 with "apologies". The working of this little sum will doubtless already be clear to the reader. 364 gross = 52 times 7 gross. 7 gross = 1008 so the multiplication sum is 52 × 1000 = 52,000 plus 52 × 8 = 416 = total 52,416. To correct the "mistake" another gross (144) was added to 52,416 making a total of 52,560 = 365 gross. A thorough acquaintance with this type of calculation enables one to work it out mentally and give an almost instantaneous answer.

In performing the above calculations, it is advisable to avoid numbers ending with cyphers such as 50 and 400 as, otherwise, a clever arithmetician in your audience may detect the secret. The larger the number that is called, the better will be the effect. With a little practice the mentalist will be able to give the answers to four- or five-figure numbers as fast as he can write them on the blackboard. It makes an effective contrast, as regards the time occupied, occasionally to get a member of the audience to prove a result at length. By way of variety a further example is given which any person of reasonable arithmetical ability should be able to perform mentally after a little training.

TONS, ETC., TO POUNDS

Write in the hundreds column the number of hundred-weights and in the tens and units columns the number of pounds. Multiply the hundred-weights by 12 and add; *i.e.* reduce 5 tons, 8 cwt., 1 qr., 7 lb., to pounds:

108 hundreds and 35 lb.	= 10835
+ 108 × 12	= 1296
	12131 lb.

TO MULTIPLY TOGETHER ANY TWO-FIGURE NUMBERS

Many years ago when endeavouring to find a short-cut in multiplication the author hit upon the method that follows. It did not come as a surprise to find later that Bidder the calculator, had already made use of exactly the same procedure in multiplying numbers.

Suppose we take 83 × 67. To clarify the description these figures will be indexed as follows:

A	B		C	D
8	3	×	6	7

First we multiply *A* by *C* (8 × 6 = 48) and to the right of this number we place the product of *B* and *D* (3 × 7 = 21). This gives us the number 4821. Next we multiply together *A* and *D* (8 × 7 = 56) and add the product of *B* and *C* (3 × 6 = 18). This gives us 74 which is placed centrally under the tens and hundreds figures of the larger number, *i.e.*

$$\begin{array}{r} 4\ 8\ 2\ 1 \\ 7\ 4 \\ \hline 5\ 5\ 6\ 1 \end{array}$$

Multiply 74 × 57. The step-by-step procedure given above will yield the following result:

$$
\begin{array}{r}
3\ 5\ ^2\ ^8 \\
6\ 9 \\
\hline
74 \times 57 = 4\ ^2\ _1\ ^8
\end{array}
$$

In using this method it is simpler to add as you go along—this was what Bidder did.

TO MULTIPLY TOGETHER ANY TWO THREE-FIGURE NUMBERS

In multiplying say, 386 × 442 the steps are as follows:

A	B	C		D	E	F
3	8	6	×	4	4	2

$A \times D = 12$, $B \times E = 32$, $C \times F = 12$. Place these
numbers alongside each other thus: 123212

Multiply	$10B \times F$ (80 × 2)	160
,,	$C \times 10E$ (6 × 40)	240
,,	$100A \times EF$ (300 × 42)	12600
,,	$100D \times BC$ (400 × 86)	34400
		170612

In actual practice this would be set out thus:

$$
\begin{array}{r}
123212 \\
40 \\
126 \\
344 \\
\hline
170612
\end{array}
$$

Two further examples:

854 × 679	483536		317 × 524	150228
	73			18
	632			72
	324			85
	579866			166108

MULTIPLICATION OF IRREGULAR LARGE SUMS OF MONEY

Rule: Treat the amount in Sterling as if it involved an ordinary multiplication sum.

Examples:

What is 94 times £63–12–7?

```
  63–12– 7
         94
 254– 10– 4  = multiplication by 4
 572 –13 –3  = multiplication of top line by 9, figures
                moved one space to the left which is
5981– 2 –10    equivalent to multiplying by 90.
```

In the above sum it will be seen that £63–12–7 is first multiplied by 4; this amount is next multiplied by 9, the figures in each case being moved one space to the left which is equivalent to multiplying £63–12–7 by 90. In adding the pence column it will be noted that we are adding 30 pence to 4 and not 3 to 4. 34d. = 2/10d.; put down 10d. and carry forward 2 to the shillings. Similarly with the shillings we add to the 10 the 2 carried forward = 12; we further add the 130 making a total of 142. We put down 2 in the shillings and carry forward £7; this 7 is added to the units column in the pounds and so on.

What is 77 times £15–17–9?

```
  15–17– 9
         77
 111– 4– 3
 111 –4 –3
1223– 6– 9
```

With a very little practice one can become accustomed to multiplying in this way, even with hundreds, and it will eventually be found much more expeditious than the old method. Suppose, for example, we wish to ascertain the value of 394 times £63–12–7.

$$
\begin{array}{r}
63\ \text{–}12\text{–}\ 7 \\
394 \\
\hline
254\text{–}\ 10\text{–}\ 4 \\
572\ \text{–}13\ \text{–}3 \\
190\ \text{–}17\text{–}\ 9 \\
\hline
25069\text{–}17\text{–}\ 10
\end{array}
$$

(Pence column totals = 934d = 77/10, put down 10d. and carry forward 77; shillings column totals 1840 plus 77 = £95-17-0, put down 17 and carry 95 to the pounds column).

Compare the above for length with the usual method which would be as follows:

$$
\begin{array}{rl}
63\text{–}12\text{–}\ 7 & (A) \\
10 \\
\hline
636\text{–}\ 5\text{–}10 & (B) = £63\text{–}12\text{–}7 \times 10 \\
10 \\
\hline
6362\text{–}18\text{–}\ 4 & (C) = £63\text{–}12\text{–}7 \times 100 \\
3 \\
\hline
19088\text{–}15\text{–}\ 0 & (D) = £63\text{–}12\text{–}7 \times 300 \\
5726\text{–}12\text{–}\ 6 & (B \times 9 = £63\text{–}12\text{–}7 \times 90) \\
254\text{–}10\text{–}\ 4 & (A \times 4 = £63\text{–}12\text{–}7 \times 4) \\
\hline
25069\text{–}17\text{–}10
\end{array}
$$

DISCOUNTS AND INTEREST

Most of the computations concerned in interest and discounts can be worked mentally if the reader will simply familiarize himself with the decimal proportions of shillings and pence to the pound. One shilling is one-twentieth of a pound, *i.e.* 0·05; a penny is 1/240th of a pound, *i.e.* 0·004.

This latter figure is approximate but it is near enough for all practical purposes where amounts are taken to the nearest penny (*see below*). £2·558 then is equivalent to £2–11–2—the first two decimal figures (·55) represent shillings and when divided by 5 = 11. The third decimal figure (8) represents pence and when divided by 4 gives 2d. £4·643 is equal to £4–12–11; £8·272 = £8–5–5½ and so on. Bearing this in mind, supposing we want to know what is 3% of £57. (Multiply 57 by 3 which gives 171). This is the equivalent of £1·71, *i.e.* £1–14–2½. (·71 divided by 5 for the shillings gives 14 with 1 to carry. This 1 is equivalent to 10 and when divided by 4 for the pence = 2½d.)

Here are further examples which the reader should have no difficulty in performing mentally:

> 7% of £33 (33 × 7 = 231) = £2·31 = £2–6–2½
> 9% of £80 (80 × 9 = 720) = £7·20 = £7–4–0
> 2½% of £67 (67 × 2½ = 167½) = £1·675 = £1–13–6
> 6¼% of £38 (38 × 6¼ = 237½) = £2·375 = £2–7–6
> 12% of £164–10 (164½ × 12 = 1974) = £19·74 = £19–14–10

It was mentioned above that 1d. is approximately 0·004 of £1. In fact, the decimal equivalent is 0·0041666 ... Where percentages higher than, say, 12½% are involved with sums exceeding, say, £12 with shillings and pence it will probably be found more expeditious not to attempt the computation mentally. Where the discount required is a multiple of any number below 12 the sum can be achieved by means of factors, for example:

35% of £17
    5% of £17 = 17 × 5 = 85 = 17/-
    35% = 7 × 17/- = £5–19–0

42% of £25

   7% of £25 = 7 × 25 = £1–15–0
   42% = 6 × £1–15–0 = £10–10–0

63% of £17–10–0

   9% of £17–10–0 = 9 × 17½ = 157½ = £1–11–6
   63% = 7 × £1–11–6 = £11–0–6

Where the required percentage is a clear fraction of 100 it is, of course, advisable to take the shortest course and divide by such a fraction. 12½% would be one-eighth of the sum involved, 25% = ¼, 33⅓% = ⅓, 37½% = ⅜, and so on. Where shillings and pence are concerned in the amount it is often quicker to compute the discount on the £'s separately, *i.e.*

7% of £6–13–4

   7% of £6 = 7 × 6 = 42 = 8/5d.
   7% of 13/4 = 7% of 160d. = 7 × 1·6 = 11d.
   8/5 plus 11d. = 9/4 which is 7% of £6–13–4

One of the shortest methods of finding the interest on any amount for a given number of days is to multiply the number of £'s by the amount of interest and divide the product by 5. The resulting figure represents the interest in *pence* for 30 days or one month. If, instead of dividing by 5 you divide by 60, the answer will show the interest in *shillings* for 30 days.

£300 @ 1% for 30 days.
   1 × 300 = 300; divide by 5 = 60d. (*Answer*)
£300 @ 3% for 30 days.
   3 × 300 = 900; divide by 60 = 15/- (*Answer*)

For two months or 60 **days double** the amount and so on.

Finally, here is a very simple method of ascertaining the number of years for any amount to double itself at any rate of compound interest: Divide the rate per cent into 72 and the answer will be the number of years it takes.

Example: How long will it take any sum of money, at 5% compound interest to double itself? 72 divided by 5 gives the answer, *i.e.* 14·4 years.

CHAPTER XVII

ARITHMETICAL RECREATIONS

Oh! My name is John Wellington Wells,
I'm a dealer in magic and spells.

W. S. GILBERT.

"IT is a pleasure to see and consider how the science of numbers doth furnish us, not only with sports to recreate the spirits, but also to bring us knowledge of admirable things"—so wrote Oughtred in his *Mathematical Recreations* published in 1653. Long before his time, however—in the sixth century B.C.—the Pythagoreans did some remarkable exploratory work on the properties of numbers, often attributing spiritual significance to the results they obtained. For instance, they laid great stress on the fact that all the numbers that will divide exactly into 6 (the divisors of 6)—namely 1, 2 and 3—themselves add up to 6. This is a rare property in numbers, the next of which it is true being 28, the divisors of which are 1, 2, 4, 7, and 14. The next three after 28 are 496, 8128 and 33,550,336. The early Pythagoreans knew only of 6 and 28 and these they called "perfect" numbers, but they had several pairs of "friendly" numbers, in which the divisors of each add up to make the other of the pair, such as 220 and 284. The divisors of 220 are 1, 2, 4, 5, 10, 11, 20, 22, 44, 55 and 110 which add up to make 284. The divisors of 284 are 1, 2, 4, 71, and 142, which add up to make 220.

The paradoxes of Zeno (490 B.C.) are still admired for their ingenuity. The best known is probably that of Achilles and the tortoise who were contestants in a race. The assertion was that if Achilles ran ten times as fast as the tortoise yet gave the tortoise (say) 1000 yards start it could never be overtaken. To establish this Zeno argued that when Achilles had gone the 1000 yards, the tortoise would still be 100 yards in front of him; by the time he had covered these 100 yards, it would still be 10 yards in front of him; and so on for ever. Thus Achilles would get nearer to the tortoise but would never overtake it.

Zeno's conclusion was that motion itself is an illusion and he further supported this contention with the following problem. If you shoot an arrow from a bow, it is in a particular position at each instant of its flight—an "instant" being defined as an infinitesimally small portion of time. Now, since the arrow's journey is made up of a succession of such instants, when does it move from each position to the next? Again, the arrow itself is an illusion, for divide it up (mentally) into an infinite number of particles, each of which will be infinitesimally small. The arrow is now being conceived as an infinite number of infinitesimally small particles; but if these particles have any size at all an infinite number of them would fill the universe. If they have no size at all, the arrow would not exist for an infinite number of nothings is still nothing! The fallacy of this argument is similar to that explained on *p.* 117.

All this tends to show there is no insuperable gulf between the paradoxes of Zeno and those of one of the greatest mathematicians of all time—Albert Einstein. Not for us these deep problems, however. Let us seek our arithmetical recreations in more simple figuring with an occasional modicum of simple deception.

NOUGHTS AND CROSSES

What could be simpler than this old game beloved of our childhood days? But perhaps not so simple as it seems! Unless both of the players have a perfect knowledge of the game, one of two things usually happens, namely, the first player wins or the game is drawn. If the first player takes the centre, the other player must take a corner, or lose. If the first player starts with a side, both must play carefully. With two experienced players, every game should be drawn.

This is a magical expression indicating that the mentalist whilst apparently giving a member of the audience a perfectly free choice of, say, a card or number is acutely forcing upon him his own (*i.e.* the mentalist's) choice.

Suppose for some reason the mentalist wishes to force, say, the number 47. Hand a slate, or pencil and paper, to a member of the audience and ask him to put down, privately, any two-figure number he wishes, between 50 and 100. The mentalist does not know the number he has written but suppose he puts down 85. Ask him to add 53 to the number he has written down. Next tell him to ignore the hundreds column in the total and to deduct the remainder from the number he first thought of. The two little sums will appear thus:

$$
\begin{array}{r}
85 \\
53 \\
\hline
138
\end{array}
\qquad
\begin{array}{r}
85 \\
38 \\
\hline
47
\end{array}
$$

It will be obvious that the mentalist's combined figures total 100 which is equivalent to the 100 discarded in the operation.

If the reader would care to develop this problem he can force two numbers on A and B respectively. When A has reached his final total, without telling the mentalist what this is, he should multiply·it by B's final number. Meanwhile, the mentalist has already handed a slip of paper to some member of the audience containing the result of this multiplication sum. If A's number was 47 and B's answer was 39 the mentalist beforehand, will have multiplied these two numbers together and the total will, of course, agree with the total of the little sum finally carried out by A or B.

A more subtle method of forcing a number, say, 672 would be to ask one member of the audience to write down any three-figure number over 700 and for another member to write underneath it any three-figure number under 300. The mentalist would then add a third row which, when added to the second row, would bring the total of these two lines to 328 (*i.e.* the difference between 1000 and the number required).

Suppose the first member of the audience writes down 847 and the second 218. The mentalist would ask for this second number and would immediately tell whoever was doing the sum to write down a third line of 110. He would then proceed as in the previous example. The sums would appear as under:

```
847
218      847
110      175
────     ───
1175     672   the number forced by mentalist
```

When once this principle has been grasped it will be found very useful as so many variations are possible.

TWO CONSECUTIVE NUMBERS

Ask A to write down any number and to get B to write down the next lower or the next higher number, without revealing these numbers to the performer. Ask A to multiply his number by two and then add B's number. Mentalist then asks for the total. Mentally divide this number by three. This will give the lower of the two numbers thought of. If, after the division by three, there is a remainder of one, then A had the lower number; if the remainder is two, then B had the lower number.

Example: Suppose that *A* thought of 65 and *B* decided to concentrate on 64. *A* doubles his number (= 130) and adds to this *B's* number of 64 = 194. This number (194) when divided by three = 64 which is the lower of the two numbers thought of. There is a remainder of 2 which proves that this was *B's* number, so that the number thought of by *A* was, of course, 65.

MULTIPLICATION BY DOUBLING

The reader may have heard of the bright little boy who could do additions without difficulty but could not multiply or divide by more than two. Despite his handicap, this same little fellow had no difficulty in multiplying together sums involving quite large numbers. Suppose he had to multiply 67 by 49. This is how his sum would appear:

67		49
33		98
16	196	
8	392	
4	784	
2	1568	
1		3136
		3283 = Answer

He doubled the multiplier and halved the multiplicand, ignoring the numbers where the halving resulted in an even figure. He added together all the numbers resulting from an odd multiplier and thus secured the required total.

EXPERIMENTS WITH A TELEPHONE DIRECTORY

Many effects can be obtained by utilizing a telephone directory in conjunction with certain basic arithmetical principles. For example, ask for any two-figure number with two different figures, reverse it and deduct the smaller from the greater. The resulting number will always cross-total to 9, *e.g.*

$$\begin{array}{r} 74 \\ 47 \\ \hline 27 \end{array} = 9$$

Any three-figure number of three different figures similarly treated will cross-total to 9 or 18. (It will usually be 18 but it *may* be 9). Example:

$$\begin{array}{r} 7\ 2\ 1 \\ 1\ 2\ 7 \\ \hline 5\ 9\ 4 \end{array} = 1\ 8$$

A four-figure number similarly treated will total 18 or 27, *e.g.*

$$\begin{array}{r} 6\ 5\ 2\ 3 \\ 3\ 2\ 5\ 6 \\ \hline 3\ 2\ 6\ 7 \end{array} = 1\ 8$$

All that the mentalist has to do is to memorize the ninth number in the first column on page nine of the telephone directory; the 18th number on page 18 and the 27th number on page 27. To prove his wonderful memory, he asks an assistant to write say, a three-figure number at random. The assistant is then instructed to reverse the number and deduct the smaller from the greater. Next he is told to cross-total the result. Assuming this cross total comes to 18, he is told to look up in the telephone directory the 18th number on page 18 which (having been previously memorized) the mentalist gives without difficulty. Care should be taken not to repeat this effect before the same audience as the possible recurrence of the cross-totals might be detected. It would be safe to give two demonstrations, however; first, with a two-figure number and then with a four-figure number.

There are other methods of forcing the numbers, 9, 18, 27 and 36. Ask the victim to write down his telephone number. Suppose this is 8721. Tell him to add a nought to the right and deduct from this larger sum his original number, *i.e.*

$$
\begin{array}{r}
8\ 7\ 2\ 1\ 0 \\
8\ 7\ 2\ 1 \\
\hline
7\ 8\ 4\ 8\ 9 = \text{cross-total } 36
\end{array}
$$

By this method a two-figure number cross-totals to 18, a three-figure number to 18 or 27, and a four-figure number to 18, 27 or 36.

WATCH-FACE PROBLEMS

In this puzzle, someone is asked to think of some hour and then to touch a number that marks another hour. For example, if he thinks of 5 and touches 9 then, if he taps successively 9, 8, 7, 6 and so on, going backwards and reckoning them respectively as 5, 6, 7, 8, etc., the tap which he reckons as 21 will be on the five.

The total number of taps, including the hour thought of, is always twelve taps more than the hour at which the taps begin. For example if you begin to tap at six o'clock and want to stop at four o'clock; you would start off at six o'clock counting four, five o'clock would be five, four o'clock would be six, three o'clock would be seven and so on, until you came to tap no. 18 (6 plus 12) which would finish at four o'clock.

There are many effects based on this principle which can be operated with numbered cards or playing cards, etc.

CHANGE FOR A SHILLING

This also is an adaptation of a very old problem. An assistant is told that he can accept IOU's from members of the audience for any amount not exceeding one shilling. He is given one shilling in coppers for "change" which change must be used to bring the value of any IOU below one shilling up to that amount. Thus, if someone hands in an IOU for 9d. the assistant gives him 3d. change from his shilling's-worth of coppers. The assistant cannot accept any IOUs involving change unless he has sufficient cash in hand to make up the amount to 1/-. Whilst the money exchanges are being effected the mentalist is either out of the room or out of sight and hearing of the transactions that are being conducted. When all is ready the mentalist appears on the scene. If there is any change left this is handed to him. He is told the number of IOUs accepted and immediately reveals the total face value of these IOUs.

Solution: The IOUs should be written on small slips of paper. Suppose there are five IOUs with 3d. change left over from the original shilling. The mentalist immediately reveals that the total amount of the IOUs is 4/3d., *i.e.* the total value of the IOUs is always one shilling less, in shillings, than the number of vouchers, plus the amount of change left over. If there were four IOUs and 7d. change the total value of the vouchers would be 3/7d.

In this example 1/- has been chosen as the maximum value of the IOUs that would be accepted. The solution would be much less likely to be detected if the maximum was increased to, say 1/3d. In this case fifteen pence would be handed to the assistant who would be told to give change for any IOU below 1/3d. When the mentalist returns to the room, suppose that 2d. change is handed to him and he is told that the assistant has six IOUs. He would answer, immediately, that the value of these

IOUs was 6/5d., *i.e.* 6 minus $1 = 5$; $5 \times 15 = 75$ plus 2
$= 6/5d.$

MAGIC ADDITION

To make the most of this effect a blackboard is desirable.
It is necessary for the mentalist to memorize three rows of
five figures each. These are permanent and it is by no means
a difficult task if one makes use of telephone numbers, etc.

Ask a member of your audience to give you any number
between 100 and 200. Suppose someone calls out 186. Write
this at the bottom of the blackboard. Request some other
person to give you any number between 100 and 1000.
Suppose this is 745. Place this to the right of the previous
number so that the line now reads 186,745. Get a member
of the audience to act as your assistant. With your back
turned ostentatiously to the blackboard call out rapidly
a five-figure number for the first line (line *A*). When this
has been written down turn towards the board and assistant
and say some such words as "Straight across the board—
that's right!" (This is really to enable the mentalist to get
another glance at the total. If he has remembered this
there is no need to turn round at all). Then call out the
next number (line *B*). Do not turn towards the board again
but call out as rapidly as can be taken down lines *C* and *D*.
Now request the assistant to total this little sum. It should
agree with the number already entered in the totals column.

Solution: The secret of this little effect lies in making the
three rows of figures *A*, *C*, and *D*, that have previously been
memorized come to a total of 111,111. The second line of
figures (row *B*) is arrived at by deducting a row of 1's
from the last five figures of the total, *i.e.* 86,745 minus
11,111 = 75,634. If desired, a more subtle key-number
than a row of 1's can be devised but the above will be
sufficient to show the possibilities of this interesting effect.

Avoid o's giving the excuse that you cannot visualize nothing!

A	51674
B	75634
C	15862
D	43575
	186745

MYSTIC DIVINATION

The mentalist, with suitable aplomb, selects a member of the audience as assistant. He then writes a message on a slip of paper, puts it in an envelope which he hands to this assistant to retain. The assistant is next instructed to cut a pack of cards as nearly as possible into two equal parts. To test the accuracy of the cut, one of the half-packs is counted and this half-pack is then handed to the assistant to hold. Another assistant is invited to take the other half-pack and to deal four lots of cards of four cards each. The assistant holding the envelope is asked to indicate any one of these four piles. The remaining three stacks are then removed. The assistant with the envelope is asked to total the numbers of the four cards he has selected. Suppose it comes to sixteen. He is instructed to count sixteen cards down the original half-pack he selected. Having located the 16th card down he is instructed to open the envelope. The number shown on the slip of paper in this envelope is identical with the particular card he selected.

Explanation: This effect depends upon a pre-arrangement of the cards. With the cards face upwards the 16th card from the top of the pack should be, say, number 32. The last 16 cards at the bottom of the pack are arranged in sets of four, each set of which totals 16, say 5, 1, 3, 7; 2, 4, 1, 9; 6, 3, 5, 2; 8, 4, 1, 3. The remainder of the cards of a pack of about 50 may be indifferent cards. The cards are cut as near as possible in the centre into two separate piles with backs up. The top portion which contains the set of 16 cards is left. The other portion with card number 32 the 16th card from the top is counted to "check the cut". This is a ruse to reverse the order of the cards in the pack. If they are checked face down the 16th card from the top will now be the 16th card from the bottom. This portion is handed to the assistant to hold. The other assistant deals out four sets of four cards from the other half of the pack (backs upwards), they should be dealt four at a time, *i.e.* one pile of four, then another and so on. One pile is selected and the remainder of the cards placed on one side. The cards in the pile now chosen will, of course, total 16 and it also follows that the 16th card in the remaining portion of the pack will correspond with the number placed in the envelope, in this example No. 32.

THREE IN A ROW

The author first made use of this effect many years ago. It involves certain well-known arithmetical principles. The originator of the problem in its present form is believed to be that famous American mathematician and mentalist, Royal Vale Heath. A member of the audience is asked to write down any three consecutive numbers below 50, without divulging these to the mentalist. Then he is instructed to add these numbers together. To the sum thus obtained, he is directed to add any number which is a multiple of 3. The resulting total he next multiplies by 67. The assistant is then requested to tell the mentalist the last two figures (tens and units) of the final sum and also the "multiple of three" number which was employed. Upon receipt of this information, the mentalist immediately reveals the three consecutive numbers and also the sum worked out by the assistant.

Solution: The "multiple of three" number is divided by 3 and 1 is added to this number. The resulting total is deducted from the "last two figures" above referred to and the answer then gives the first of the three consecutive numbers. The total of the sum will be the "tens and units" number already revealed and to the left of these figures, in the hundreds and thousands columns, twice the number given for the "tens and units". Like many of these descriptions, the sum appears to be somewhat involved but it is really extremely simple in operation.

Suppose the assistant out of the audience selects the consecutive numbers 27, 28 and 29. These three numbers total 84. Suppose he adds 15 for the "multiple of three" number. The total is now 99. This number is multiplied by 67, *i.e.* 99 × 67 = 6633. The figures revealed to the performer are the last two in this number (*i.e.* 33) and the "multiple of three" number (*i.e.* 15). The mentalist divides 15 by 3 and adds 1 (= 6). This 6 is deducted from 33, leaving 27—the first of the three consecutive numbers so the other two must, of course, be 28 and 29. The mentalist already knows the last two numbers of the addition sum (*i.e.* 33) and the first two figures are double that number, *i.e.* 66, making the total 6633.

Now let us assume that the three consecutive numbers are 12, 13 and 14 and the "multiple of three" number is 27. These, when added, give a total of 66. When this is multiplied by 67 we get 4422. The "multiple of three" number is 27. Divided by 3 this yields 9 and 1 is added, which leaves 10 to be taken from 22 = 12. Thus we get 12 for the first of the three consecutive numbers, whilst the total of the sum is 22, preceded by a number double that amount, *i.e.* 44 = 4422. If he cares to do so, by exercising his ingenuity, the mentalist can so camouflage his requests for the information he requires, as to render these quite innocuous and so increase the bewilderment of his audience.

The basic effect also lends itself to development and modification.

THE THREE PILE PROBLEM

The origin of this problem is lost in obscurity. It is mentioned by Bachet but was current before his time. This is yet another puzzle where the principles involved lend themselves to various modifications and the mentalist could profitably devote his skill to the discovery of fresh routines. In this effect, the mentalist discovers which card an assistant (member of his audience) is thinking of. The trick is usually performed as follows. Take 27 cards and deal them into three piles with the faces upwards. By "dealing" is to be understood that the top card of the pack of 27 is placed as the bottom card of the first pile; the second card in the pack as the bottom card of the second pile; the third card as the bottom card of the third pile; the fourth card on the top of the first card in the first pile and so on. Throughout the problem it is assumed that the cards are held by the mentalist with the faces upwards. Modifications may be introduced to cover other methods of dealing.

Method: The mentalist asks a spectator to note any card and remember in which pile it is put. After completing the deal, the mentalist asks the spectator to indicate the pile containing the selected card. This pile is placed between the other two and the cards are again set out as before. Once again the spectator indicates the pile containing his card and, for the second time, this pile is placed between the other two. The same routine is followed for a third time but on this occasion the mentalist makes a note of the middle card of each pile. This time, the middle card of the pile indicated by the spectator is the card he thought of.

If preferred, the cards can be placed together as previously, for the third time and thirteen cards counted mentally from the top or bottom of the pack as desired. In this case, the middle (fourteenth) card will be the one thought of. For an appropriate finale, the mentalist should have no difficulty in employing his wits to invent a more subtle solution than the somewhat clumsy methods indicated above.

ELIMINATION

A pack of playing cards is handed to a member of the audience. He is instructed to shuffle these and arrange them in any order he desires. He is next told to place the cards in heaps of twelve, this number being made up of cards and spots combined. If, for example, he places a six of hearts *face downwards* he adds any six cards from the pack to make the total twelve in all. Ace counts as 1 and all court cards as 10. If the first card in any pile is, say, the ace of clubs then another eleven cards must be added to same. This procedure is followed until the cards are exhausted or until the cards left over are insufficient to make a pile of twelve. Suppose there are seven piles and three odd cards left over. The performer, who has been out of the room or away from the table at which the operations have been conducted, at a glance and without touching the cards will accurately name the total number of spots on the top cards of the seven piles laid face down. In this particular instance the number would be 42.

Solution: Forget four of the piles. Multiply the remainder of the piles by 13 and add the odd cards left over. The above illustration mentions seven piles with three odd cards left over. Four of the piles deducted from a total of seven leaves 3; 3×13 plus $3 = 42$. If the cards are set out the method employed will always be infallibly accurate. Note carefully that it is the total number of spots on the face (or top) cards of the "twelves" packs that is forecast; that four piles are deducted from the total number of such piles; that the balance of piles left over is multiplied by 13 and that to the resulting total, the number of odd cards (NOT the spots on these cards) must be added.

For want of a more expressive term, this effect has been named "Elimination", *i.e.* the twelves are eliminated from the pack and the whole secret lies in the number of cards left over plus the number of piles of twelves. There is, however, no necessity to set out the complete pack. Suppose, for example, in the above description, the cards in any one pile are picked up and placed with the cards left over. Say the card in this pile was five of diamonds; there would then be eight cards in all to add to those left over. There would now be left six piles and eleven cards over. Four from six leaves 2; 2 × 13 plus 11 = 37 = total value of the face cards in all the piles.

Suppose three piles only are laid down, the face cards consisting of the 5 of spades, 10 of hearts and 2 of diamonds respectively. The total face value will, of course, be 17. We shall thus have three piles and thirty cards left over. In this case we *subtract* 13 from 30 leaving 17 which is the correct answer. If only two piles are employed we should deduct two times thirteen from the number of cards left over and so on.

MODIFIED METHOD OF PRESENTING "ELIMINATION"

This effect is improved if, instead of stacking the selected cards in sets of twelve, one card only is turned down for each pile, the balance of the cards from such piles being all put together in a separate heap. For example, if the cards selected had face values of 4, 4, 8, 9, 10, 5, 1 there would, in addition to the cards turned over, be two separate piles—one consisting of 43 cards and the other of the two cards left over. Suppose an apparently careless glance at the two cards over revealed an ace and a ten. We know that the spots on the seven cards turned down come to a total of 41. The spots on the ace and the ten come to 11.

The mentalist turning to the assistant and pointing to the heap of cards left over from the "twelveses" says: "If you care to count the spots on the cards in that pile you will find that they total 288". The method of arriving at this number of 288 will be fairly obvious—the total number of pips in a pack of 52 cards, where an ace counts as 1 and a court card as 10, is 340. The cards turned down in the present example total 41; the spots on the two odd cards total 11, making 52 in all which when deducted from 340 leaves 288.

The principles involved in "Elimination" provide plenty of scope for developing special effects. The subtraction and multiplying factors will, of course, vary according to the numbering and the quantity of cards employed. Thus, if cards of one suit only are employed, instead of ignoring four of the piles laid out we should ignore one pile only. if two suits are employed we deduct two from the piles before multiplying by thirteen and so on.

ASTRONOMICAL FIGURES

To conclude this chapter here are two simple questions that it is suggested, should be employed as test questions for calculators! The first is: "What would be the total thickness of a sheet of paper, one-thousandth of an inch thick, folded over double 56 times?" The sum is by no means formidable but the answer is truly amazing. It is:

1,137,272,633 miles, 306 yards, 2 feet, 7.936 inches.

The second test is to state how many combinations are possible with 24 letters of the alphabet, no particular letter appearing more than once in an individual combination, *i.e.* the longest combinations to consist of 24 letters and the shortest of one letter? The answer (if there is no mistake in the arithmetic!) is that up to 24 letters can be varied no fewer than 620,448,593,438,860,623,360,000 times.

CHAPTER XVIII

MAGIC SQUARES

I have not kept the square,
But that to come,
Shall all be done by the rule.

ANTONY AND CLEOPATRA. *Act* I, *iii.*

N o résumé of mental magic would be complete without some reference to magic squares which, in China, date back to some 3000 years B.C. They have long intrigued both

FIGURE I

8	1	6
3	5	7
4	9	2

= 15

mentalists and calculators, probably because the principles of their construction are simple to grasp and also because the rapid formation of a magic square has a most impressive effect on the uninstructed ónlooker. A magic square consists of a series of numbers arranged in quadratic form so that the sum of each vertical, horizontal and main diagonal line is always the same. It is beyond the scope of this book to do other than refer to a few of the simpler forms of magic squares.

It may be noted that the actual shape of the 'squares' is not vital provided that they are rectangles.

The smallest aggregation of numbers capable of arrangement in magic square form is shown in figure I.

The smallest even magic square is the four-sided example in figure II.

There are at least 4352 diverse forms of four-sided magic squares that can be constructed with the numbers 1 to 16

FIGURE II

1	15	14	4
12	6	7	9
8	10	11	5
13	3	2	16

= 34

and, up to a few years ago, at all events, nobody could assert with any authority in how many ways it was possible to form a magic square of any order exceeding four by four. It is no exaggeration to claim that some of the larger squares can be arranged in millions of different ways.

The usual arrangement for a simple four-sided magic square is indicated by figure III, consisting of moves combining those of the knight and castle in chess.

1			
		2	
4			
		3	

a

	8		
			7
	5		
			6

b

			12
	11		
			9
	10		

c

		13	
14			
		16	
15			

d

FIGURE III

The formula is simple: Let F represent the required first figure and S the desired constant; then for a four-sided square this would be $F = \frac{S - 30}{4}$. Example: for a total of 1934, $F = \frac{1934 - 30}{4} = 476$ (*see* figure IV).

476	483	488	487
489	486	477	482
479	480	491	484
490	485	478	481

FIGURE IV   = 1934

The five-sided square is probably the simplest and most effective from the point of view of the mentalist. This will cover columns totalling from 60 to 500. To obtain the lowest figure, deduct 60 from the number chosen and divide by 5; *i.e.* for a total of 65, then $65 - 60 = 5$ which when divided by 5 gives 1 as the lowest number (*see* figure V).

17	24	1	8	15
23	5	7	14	16
4	6	13	20	22
10	12	19	21	3
11	18	25	2	9

FIGURE V   = 65

Begin with the first figure in the centre of the top line and proceed diagonally upwards to the right. Imagine that it is possible to arrange the square in cylindricla form in both directions. Then, proceeding diagonally upwards to the right for filling 2, we actually come to the second square from the right, on the bottom line. Where the next figure upwards and diagonally to the right is occupied and the square underneath is free, take that for the next number. For example, travelling from 5 to 6, the next square diagonally after 5 is occupied by 1 but the square underneath 5 is free, so take that for the next number. Filling in the squares becomes purely automatic, after a little practice.

Where the required number, after 60 has been deducted, is not exactly divisible by 5, it is necessary to add or subtract the remainder to certain key squares. Take for example, the number 248 (figure VI). $248 - 60 = 188$, $\div 5 = 37$ with a remainder of 3. In this case, assuming that we start with the number 37, it will be necessary to add 3 to the numbers which would ordinarily appear in the key squares. Alternatively, we can begin with 38 and deduct 2 from the numbers ordinarily appearing in the key squares. The positions of the key squares are indicated in figure VI by asterisks. Until he has become used to these key positions the mentalist is advised to mark the blank key squares beforehand.

FIGURE VI

52	61	38	45	52
60	42	42 *	51	53
41	43	50	57	57 *
47	47 *	56	58	40
48	55	62	37 *	46

= 248

Kraitchik's *Mathematical Recreations* (Bib. 17) gives detailed methods of construction of many types of magic squares, from the simple to the complex.

SECTION V

PSYCHOLOGICAL ASPECTS

CHAPTER XIX

SUBCONSCIOUS OR UNCONSCIOUS?

When Nature has work to be done,
She creates a genius to do it.
RALPH WALDO EMERSON.

"SUBCONSCIOUS" is generally used as indicating those thoughts and feelings, etc., beneath the ordinary threshold of consciousness. This definition is equally well applied to the word "subliminal".

Freud and his followers give to the word "unconscious" a meaning described by Dr. Ernest Jones as "a region of the mind, the content of which is characterized by the attribute of being repressed, conative, instinctive, infantile, unreasoning and predominantly sexual. . . . The existence of the unconscious is the result of repression".

The battle between the adherents of the "subconscious" theories and the exponents of the "unconscious" theories continues to be waged with undiminished energy. With the employment of so many different words, with so many similar and different meanings, in the attempt to explain a certain state of mind it is not remarkable that ordinary individuals should, at times, become hopelessly befogged, so we will stick to "subconscious".

The reader may reasonably enquire as to the connection (if any) between the Daemon of Socrates and the marvels performed by calculating boys, memory "fiends", chess and musical prodigies, and the like. The reply is that these various phases are usually associated with the activities of the subconscious mind. The mathematical prodigy with no conscious effort on his part, is frequently able to give an answer to an intricate arithmetical problem through, or via, the subconscious mind.

How far is this subconscious mind "all-knowing"? Is it simply the storehouse of all that has happened to the conscious mind or can it initiate and bring to the surface matters which have never come within the ken of the conscious? It is something bordering on the miraculous for an illiterate child to give immediately the answer to a complicated sum the solution of which might occupy an educated man for several hours and in attempting to answer the questions we have set ourselves, we are treading on difficult ground.

It is frequently claimed that everything we have ever seen, or sensed in any form, is automatically recorded in the subconscious mind. This attitude was developed by Thomson Jay Hudson who said: "One of the most striking and important peculiarities of the subjective mind, as distinguished from the objective, consists in its prodigious memory. It would perhaps be hazardous to say that the memory of the subjective mind is perfect but there is good ground for believing that such a proposition would be substantially true."

Referring to the study of arithmetical prodigies Myers, in his *Human Personality* (Bib. 4) considered it a special advantage that, in their case, "the subjective impression coincides closely with the objective result. The subliminal computer feels that the sum is right, and it is right. Forms of real or supposed genius which are more interesting are apt to be less undeniable."

Myers goes on to say that an American (Professor Scripture) and a French psychologist (Professor Binet) have collected such hints and explanations as these prodigies have given of their methods of working; methods which one might naturally hope to find useful in ordinary education. The result, however, has been very meagre and the records left to us, imperfect as they are, are enough to show that the main and primary achievement has, in fact, been subliminal. Conscious or supraliminal effort has sometimes been wholly absent; sometimes has supervened only after the gift has been so long exercised that the accesses between different strata have become easy by frequent traversing. The prodigy, grown to manhood, who now recognizes the arithmetical artifices which he used unconsciously as a boy, resembles the hypnotic subject trained by suggestion to remember, in waking hours, the events of the trance.

Myers continues: "In almost every point, indeed, where comparison is possible, we shall find this computative gift resembling other manifestations of subliminal faculty—such as the power of seeing hallucinatory figures—rather than the results of steady supraliminal effort, such as the power of logical analysis. In the first place, this faculty, in spite of its obvious connection with general mathematical grasp and insight, is found almost at random—among non-mathematical and even quite stupid persons, as well as among mathematicians of mark. In the second place, it shows itself mostly in early childhood, and tends to disappear in later life: in this resembling visualizing power in general, and the power of seeing hallucinatory figures in particular; which powers, as both Mr. Galton's enquiries and our own tend to show, are habitually stronger in childhood and youth than in later years. Again, it is noticeable that when the power disappears early in life it is apt to leave behind it no memory whatever of the processes involved. And even when, by long persistence in a reflective mind, the power has become, so to say, adopted into the supraliminal consciousness, there nevertheless may still be flashes of pure 'inspiration' when the answer 'comes into the mind' with absolutely no perception of intermediate steps."

Now let us see what Myers has to say concerning Socrates —the Founder of Science. Socrates—the permanent type of sanity, shrewdness, physical robustness and moral balance was guided in all his affairs by a monitory, inward voice— by "the Daemon of Socrates". With that simplicity of diction, which is so typical of Myers, he says: "This is a case which can never lose its interest, a case which has been vouched for by the most practical, and discussed by the loftiest intellect of Greece, both of them intimate friends of the illustrious subject; a case, therefore, where one who endeavours to throw new light on hallucination and automatism is bound, even at this distant time, to endeavour to explain. And this is the more needful, since a treatise was actually written, a generation ago . . . arguing from the records in Xenophon and Plato that Socrates was, in fact, insane.

"I believe that it is now possible to give a truer explanation . . . and to show that the messages which Socrates received were only advanced examples of a process which, if supernormal, is not abnormal and which characterizes that form of intelligence which we describe as genius. The story of Socrates I take as a signal example of wise automatism; of the possibility that the messages that are conveyed to the supraliminal mind from subliminal strata of the personality—whether as sounds, as sights, or as movements —may sometimes come from far beneath the realm of dream or confusion—from some self whose monitions convey to us a wisdom profounder than we know."

Professor C. G. Seligman (Bib. 34) has very similar ideas to those put forward by Myers. He says: "The first idea I shall ask you to accept is that unconscious mental processes occur; for instance, many of us can set ourselves to wake at an unusually early hour if we have a train to catch, whilst some can wake with remarkable precision, showing there is a more or less accurate appreciation of time during sleep, though clearly this is not conscious. It is generally held that a large part of our mind is made up of these unconscious mental processes, indeed conscious and unconscious have been compared respectively with the parts of an iceberg, about one-eighth above water (consciousness) and seven-eighths below (unconsciousness)."

In the book quoted above (Bib. 34) Dame Edith Lyttleton carries the argument a step further. She writes: "It is the unconscious part of our minds which has the greatest power and not only over our bodies. It possesses a far wider range than we realize, and can gather information of events, in the past or at a distance, or even in the future. I have said nothing about the visions and intuitions of poets or the inspiration and teaching of religious mystics, yet these great expressions of the human mind point in the same direction, namely, towards the reality of another world with which we occasionally experience contact. If you read the description given by poets, artists, musicians, scientific inventors, mathematicians, you will find many who feel that their ideas come to them from outside and that there has been no conscious effort of thought but a sudden understanding or idea, even if only a germ, which they can consciously work upon afterwards. I believe these flashes of inspiration reach the conscious mind through that part of the mind which I call the superconscious and which has contact with other worlds of being."

CHAPTER XX

SPECULATIONS AND CONCLUSIONS

*Though I throw out my speculations to entertain the
learned and metaphysical world, yet in other things I do not
think so differently from the rest of the world as you imagine.*

DAVID HUME.

W E are approaching the conclusion of our brief account
of the wonders and frailties of human prodigies and may
pause to consider how our findings affect the practical
problems of philosophy and every-day life.

The first thing we learn is that the ability to figure, or
even a good memory, is not necessarily accompanied by
intellectual acuteness, nor does the growth of memory, of
necessity, accompany intellectual advancement. Brains do
not enter into the matter of counting and education has
frequently destroyed the gift. Again—and we are generaliz-
ing now—we get an impression of a lack of balance on the
part of many of these prodigies. They cannot have it every
way.

Even so, prodigies *have* probably served some useful
purpose. The calculating boy, Zerah Colburn, was the
instrument for directing the energies of Sir William Hamilton
to those branches of mathematics and science, in which he
eventually excelled. Hamilton's reference to Colburn's
influence occurs in a letter written in August, 1882, when he
was seventeen. It relates how he and Colburn were brought
together in the hope that he would be able to assist the
American boy in finding some explanation of his arithmetical
ability.

It was the same Sir William Hamilton who referred to
"acts of mind so rapid and minute as to elude the ken of
consciousness". It would hardly be possible to obtain a

better answer to the question "How do you do it?" so often put to calculators and so often evaded or answered "I don't know!" They do not know because the mental operations are so rapid as to elude "the ken of consciousness". It was only the more intellectual type, like Bidder, who independently reached a conclusion similar to this.

The nearest approach to the natural calculator, as opposed to the trained mentalist, is the subject under hypnosis. From experience, the author is convinced that hypnotized persons are able to calculate far more quickly and accurately than in their normal condition. There is further evidence that such subjects have a very accurate time-sense.

Let us refer again to the experiment conducted by Dr. J. Milne Bramwell (*p.* 114). A lady subject, whilst in the hypnotic sleep, was told that at the expiration of 11,470 minutes from the time of awakening she would put a cross on paper and note the time. This was duly carried out and Milne Bramwell reports that out of 55 such experiments some 45 were completely successful. Professor Bernheim also gives particulars of a similar case (*see p.* 115).

In estimating the passage of, say, 470 minutes it is necessary to know how long a minute lasts and to estimate 470 such periods. We have all more or less, an accurate idea of time as indicated say, by the hands of a watch. We know what we did approximately one hour ago or even a week ago. Many of us by an effort of will can awake at a given time in the morning.

Whence do we derive this time and counting sense? May it not be obtained from the regular rhythmic action of certain bodily processes? There are several such but we will confine ourselves to the two most conspicuous. Throughout the whole of our life, like the regular throb of an engine, the human heart beats at a fairly uniform rate and the same applies to the process of breathing. In the event of any noticeable variation, the brain is immediately aware that something is wrong caused, say, by palpitation or bronchitis.

The evidence produced for the reality of constitutional rhythms and the knowledge of a time-sense, will now be applied to the question of calculation. In each of the processes referred to, counting is an essential feature. Counting and calculation, for the purpose of the argument, are near enough alike. It can reasonably be claimed that calculation is as natural a function as hearing, smelling, tasting and seeing. It is not necessary to claim a sixth or even seventh sense—the sense of time or counting. It is part and parcel of the sense of feeling.

The counting sense is inborn in each one of us and is not restricted to human beings—certain animals have a sense of time and the ability to count up to small numbers. Without conscious effort, a person is able to calculate the passing of 11,470 minutes. Is this less wonderful than the ability of a boy, with no particular intelligence apart from a good figure-memory, being able to calculate? Is not any difference there may be, one of degree only? Counting can be instinctive in that it can be carried out without reasoning or conscious design. Is this an answer to the question: "How does a calculating boy calculate?"

TALLY-STICKS

The English tally has many historical associations. It was used as an expense voucher from the days of the Conqueror, the amounts being indicated by notches of various types, with names and details written on the sides in ink. The stick measures about six inches long and those used by the Exchequer were shaped like a small oar. It was usual for the token to be split in two, one half being retained by the Exchequer and the other portion going to the payee as a receipt.

The system was abolished by an Act of 1782 but it was not actually discontinued until the death of the last of the Chamberlains in 1826. These tallies were stored in the Star Chamber which was filled to overflowing and when, in 1834, it was desired to use the room for other purposes they were ordered to be burned. The instructions were carried out with so much zeal and indiscretion that the stoves became red-hot and ignited the peers' benches. The fire spread rapidly and with the exception of Westminster Hall, the old Houses of Parliament were burned down and a precious relic of six centuries of England's history was destroyed.

Charles Dickens in an address to the Administrative Reform Association at the Theatre Royal, Drury Lane on 27 June, 1855, was at the top of his bent in ridiculing this "savage" mode of keeping accounts. This is what he had to say (*The Nonesuch Dickens*, Vol 2, *pp.* 415–423).

"Ages ago a savage mode of keeping accounts on notched sticks was introduced into the Court of Exchequer and the accounts were kept much as Robinson Crusoe kept his calendar on the desert island. A multitude of accountants, book-keepers, and actuaries were born and died. Still official routine inclined to those notched sticks as if they were pillars of the Constitution, and still the Exchequer accounts continued to be kept on certain splints of elm-wood called *tallies*. In the reign of George III an enquiry was made by some revolutionary spirit whether pens, ink and paper, slates and pencils being in existence, this obstinate adherence to an obsolete custom ought to be continued, and whether a change ought not to be effected. All the red tape in the country grew redder at the bare mention of this bold and original conception, and it took until 1826 to get these sticks abolished. In 1834 it was found that there was a considerable accumulation of them; and the question then arose, what was to be done with such worn-out, worm-eaten, rotten old bits of wood? The sticks were housed in Westminster, and it would naturally occur to any intelligent person that nothing could be easier than to allow them to be carried away for firewood by the miserable people who live in that neighbourhood. However, they never had been useful, and official routine required that they never should be, and so the order went out that they were to be privately and confidentially burned. It came to pass that they were burned in a stove in the House of Lords. The stove, over-gorged with these preposterous sticks, set fire to the panelling, the panelling set fire to the House of Commons; the two houses were reduced to ashes; architects were called in to build others; and we are now in the second million of the cost thereof."

In the Birmingham Public Library there is an excellent collection of sixty-seven wooden Exchequer and other tallies. On many of these are to be found inscriptions in Hebrew, suggesting that many of the "customers" were of that persuasion. The collection includes specimen tallies in use among shop-keepers and agricultural workers. It is claimed that they were being used by hop pickers as late as 1903. The reason for the popularity of this primitive method of keeping accounts is, of course, to be found in the fact that they were easily understood by the illiterate and all who had no knowledge of other methods of figuring.

APPENDIX II

BACHET'S "THINK OF A NUMBER"

C. G. BACHET, in his classical *Problèmes plaisans et délectables*, (*p.* 87 of the 1624 edition) refers to the previous history of this problem. It is also dealt with at some length by W. W. Rouse Ball, on pages 7 and 8 of the 1892 edition of his *Mathematical Recreations and Problems* (Bib. 38), as follows:

Ask any one to select a number less than 60. (i) Request him to divide it by 3 and mention the remainder; suppose it to be a. (ii) Request him to divide it by 4, and mention the remainder; suppose it to be b. (iii) Request him to divide it by 5 and mention the remainder; suppose it to be c. Then the number selected is the remainder obtained by dividing $40a + 45b + 36c$ by 60.

This method can be generalized and then will apply to any number chosen. Let a', b', c', . . . be a series of numbers prime to one another, and let p be their product. (The rule given by Bachet applies to the case of the three numbers, 3, 4, 5.) Let n be any number less than p, and let a, b, c, . . . be the remainders when n is divided by a', b', c', . . . respectively. Find a number A which is a multiple of the product $b'c'd'$ . . . and which exceeds by unity a multiple of a'. Find a number B which is a multiple of $a'c'd'$ . . . and which exceeds by unity a multiple of b'; and similarly find analogous numbers C, D, . . . I proceed to show that n is equal to the remainder when $Aa + Bb + Cc$ is divided by p. Let $N = Aa + Bb + Cc + . . .$ and let $M(x)$ stand for a multiple of x.

Then $A = M(a') + 1$, and therefore $Aa = M(a')a + a$. Hence if the first term in N, that is Aa, is divided by a', the remainder is a.

Again, B is a multiple of $a'c'd'$ . . . Therefore Bb is exactly divisible by a'. Similarly Cc, Dd, . . . are each exactly divisible by a'. Hence every term in N, except the first, is exactly divisible by a'.

Hence, if N is divided by a', the remainder is a, but   if n is divided by a', the remainder is a.
Therefore $N - n = M(a')$.
Similarly $N - n = M(b')$.
             $N - n = M(c')$.
But a', b', c', . . . are prime to one another.
Therefore, $N - n = M(a'b'c' . .) = M(p)$,
that is $N = M(p) + n$.

Now n is less than p, hence, if N is divided by p, the remainder is n.

In general, if the numbers a', b', c', . . . are small, the corresponding numbers A, B, C, . . . can be found by inspection. The rule given by Bachet corresponds to the case of $a' = 3$, $b' = 4$, $c' = 5$, $p = 60$, $A = 40$, $B = 45$, $C = 36$. If the number chosen is less than 420, we may take $a = 3$, $b = 4$, $c = 5$, $d = 7$, $A = 280$, $B = 105$, $C = 336$, $D = 120$.

APPENDIX III

(*See* Zerah Colburn, *pages* 23 *and* 26)

A MATHEMATICAL friend calls attention to the fact that although a number like 999 looks very difficult to multiply by, it is in fact one of the easiest. For example, Colburn's problem (*p.* 26) of squaring 999,999. Using the formula $(a - b)^2 = a^2 + b^2 - 2\,ab$, $999,999^2$, which is $(1,000,000 - 1)^2$ is simply

$$
\begin{array}{r}
1,000,000,000,000 \\
+ \qquad\qquad\qquad 1 \\
- \qquad\quad 2,000,000 \\
\hline
999,998,000,001
\end{array}
$$

Another "figure-friend" supplies the interesting information that raising a number consisting only of 9's to the 2nd, 3rd, 4th, and 5th powers involves nothing more than memorizing 9^2, 9^3, 9^4, 9^5, after which the answers can be written down. Strangely enough, this system breaks down at higher powers than the 5th. The following example will make the system clear:

What is the value of 9999^2?

Answer: Write down the square of 9 ($= $ **81**) leaving a space between the digits. Then in front of the **8** write a series of 9's one less in number than the number of 9's to be squared. In the example given there are four 9's, therefore, we write down *three* in front of the **8**.

Between the **8** and the **1**, write down the *same* number of 0's; the result is 999**8**000**1** which equals 9999^2. Similarly, $99999^2 = 9999$**8**0000**1**.

APPENDIX IV *(See page* 91*)*

ROMAN NUMERALS

I	.	.	. 1	LXX	.	.	70
II	.	.	. 2	LXXX	.	.	80
III	.	.	. 3	LXXXVIII	.		88
IV	.	.	. 4	XC .	.	.	90
V	.	.	. 5	XCIX	.	.	99
VI	.	.	. 6	C .	.	.	100
VII	.	.	. 7	CX .	.	.	110
VIII	.	.	. 8	CXI	.	.	111
IX	.	.	. 9	CXC	.	.	190
X	.	.	. 10	CC .	.	.	200
XI	.	.	. 11	CCXX	.	.	220
XII	.	.	. 12	CCXXIV	.		224
XIII	.	.	. 13	CCC	.	.	300
XIV	.	.	. 14	CCCXX	.	.	320
XV	.	.	. 15	CD .	.	.	400
XVI	.	.	. 16	D .	.	.	500
XVII	.	.	. 17	DC .	.	.	600
XVIII	.	.	. 18	DCCC	.	.	800
XIX	.	.	. 19	DCCCLXXVI	.		876
XX	.	.	. 20	CM .	.	.	900
XXX	.	.	. 30	CMXCIX	.		999
XL	.	.	. 40	M .	.	.	1000
L	.	.	. 50	MD	.	.	1500
LV	.	.	. 55	MDCCC	.	.	1800
LX	.	.	. 60	MM	.	.	2000

The reader may care to exercise his ingenuity in multiplying, in Roman numerals, say, LXXXVIII (88) by DCCCLXXVI (876).

BIBLIOGRAPHY

Most of the books in the following list are referred to in the text—occasionally at some length. For this privilege the author wishes again to mention his indebtedness to the authors and publishers concerned.

Ref.
Bib. No.

1. Cleveland, Alfred A.—The Psychology of Chess. *American Journal of Psychology*, Vol. XVIII, 1907.
2. Scripture, Dr. E. W.—Arithmetical Prodigies. *American Journal of Psychology*, Vol. IV, 1891.
3. Mitchell, Dr. Frank D.—Mathematical Prodigies. *American Journal of Psychology*, Vol. XVIII, 1907.
4. Myers, F. W. H.—*Human Personality*. Longmans Green & Co. Ltd., 1913. (By kind permission of Mr. Harold Myers.)
5. Colburn, Zerah.—*A Memoir of Zerah Colburn*. Written by himself. Springfield, Mass. 1833.
6. Bidder, George—*Proceedings of the Institution of Civil Engineers*. Vols. XV, 1855–6 and LVII, 1878–9
7. Chambers *Edinburgh Journal*, 1847.
8. *Spectator*. Vol. LI, 1878: Vol. LII, 1879.
9. *Gentleman's Magazine*. 1751, Vol. XXI: 1753, Vol. XXIII: 1754, Vol. XXIV.
10. *The Annual Register*. 20 August, 1812.
11. *British Journal of Psychical Research*. Vol. I, No. 12, 1928.
12. Russell, A. H.—*Rapid Calculations*. Gregg Publishing Co. Ltd., 1944.
13. Binet, Professor—*Psychologie des grands Calculateurs et joueurs d'échecs*, 1894.
14. Heath, R. Vale—*Mathemagic*. New York.
15. Carrel, Dr. Alexis—*Man, the Unknown*. Penguin, 1948.
16. Collection *Sciences Métapsychiques*, Cahier III, 1947.
17. Kraitchik, Maurice—*Mathematical Recreations*. Geo. Allen & Unwin Ltd., 1943.
18. Tyrrell, G. N. M.—*The Personality of Man*. Pelican, 1948.
19. Gregory, J. C.—*Mind*, n.s. XXV.
20. *Popular Science Monthly*. September, 1936.

21. Wood, Professor Ernest E.—*Mind and Memory Training.* Pitman.
22. Pear, T. H., M.A., B.SC.—*Remembering and Forgetting.* Methuen.
23. Bankoff, Dr. George—*The Conquest of Brain Mysteries.* Macdonald & Co. Ltd.
24. Bankoff, Dr. George—*The Story of the Endocrine Glands.* Macdonald & Co. Ltd.
25. Rhine, J. B.—*New Frontiers of the Mind.* Faber & Faber Ltd.
26. Dunne, J. W.—*An Experiment with Time.* Faber & Faber Ltd., 1939.
27. Hadfield, J. A.—*Psychology and Mental Health.* Geo. Allen & Unwin Ltd.
28. Hoyle, Fred—*The Nature of the Universe.* Basil Blackwell.
29. *Encyclopaedia of Psychic Science.* Dr. Nandor Fodor. Arthurs Press Ltd.
30. Berg, Dr. Louis—*The Human Personality.* Williams & Norgate Ltd.
31. Galton, Francis—*Hereditary Genius.* C. A. Watts & Co. Ltd.
32. Hamilton, Sir William—*Lectures on Metaphysics.*
33. Bell, Dr. E. T.—*Men of Mathematics.* Victor Gollancz Ltd.
34. *Enquiry into the Unknown.* Edited by T. Besterman. Methuen.
35. Carington, Whately—*Matter, Mind and Meaning.* Methuen.
36. Whiteley, G. H., M.A.—*An Introduction to Metaphysics.* Methuen.
37. Andrews, W. A. (U.S.A.)—*Magic Squares and Cubes.*
38. Ball, W. W. Rouse—*Mathematical Recreations & Problems.* Macmillan & Co., 1892.
39. *"Datas" the Memory Man,* by himself (W. J. M. Bottle). Wright & Brown.

Thankful acknowledgment is also made for permission to quote from the *Sunday Express*, the *News Chronicle*, the *Birmingham Mail*, the *Radio Times*, the *Listener* and *John O' London's Weekly*.

INDEX